RATIOS OF STAFF TO USERS
Implications for library-information work and the potential for automation

Margaret Slater

Aslib Occasional Publication No 24

© 1981 Aslib
3 Belgrave Square, London SW1X 8PL

ISBN 0 85142 144 X

A study of the special sector of the library-information field. Coverage includes: staff to user ratios (normative and "ideal"); staff and user population structures; quantitative and qualitative adequacy of current staffing; traffic analysis; automation potential. Data was collected by questionnaire distributed late October 1979. The project was carried out at Aslib and funded by the British Library Research and Development Department.

Aslib Research & Consultancy Division
August 1980

Printed in Great Britain by Unwin Brothers Limited, Old Woking, Surrey GU22 9LH

Contents

		Page
1.	**Why and How Staffing Ratios were Studied (introduction)**	1
1.1	Aims and scope	1
1.2	Justification or rationale for such work	2
1.3	Methodology and detailed aims	4
2.	**Summary**	6
2.1	Published statistics as a ratio source	6
2.2	Ratios emerging directly from this study	7
2.3	Services and their titles: What's in a name?	9
2.4	Staffing structures	10
2.5	Doomwatch scenario: A shrinking profession?	12
2.6	Staffing adequacy: Size and composition	12
2.7	Current ways of assessing staffing levels	13
2.8	User populations	14
2.9	Personpower alternatives: Automation	16
3.	**Any Relevant Data Publicly Available?**	18
4.	**Ratios: Data and Comment**	27
4.1	Normative staff to user ratios	28
4.2	"Ideal" ratios	34
4.3	Workload ratios	36
5.	**The Services**	37
5.1	Descriptive data (sample composition)	37
5.2	Formal service title versus actual function	43
6.	**Staffing Structures**	45
6.1	Staff size and composition	45
6.2	Mismatch between posts and qualifications	53
6.3	Part-time or full-time?	56
7.	**A Shrinking Profession?**	59
7.1	Frozen posts	59
7.2	Growth or attrition?	61
8.	**Adequacy of Current Staffing**	62
8.1	Quantitative adequacy	62
8.2	Qualitative adequacy	64

9.	**Assessment of Staffing Needs: Current Practice**	69
9.1	How satisfactory are current methods?	69
9.2	What methods are used?	69
9.3	Any usage of ratio methods?	73
10.	**Users in General**	78
10.1	Actual, potential and theoretically possible users	78
10.2	Onsite and offsite users	80
11.	**Onsite Users**	85
11.1	Broad parameters of potential user definition	85
11.2	Service bias in user definition	86
11.3	Privilege and deprivation: In-groups and out-groups	88
11.4	Reliability or hardness of onsite numerical data	90
12.	**Offsite Users**	96
12.1	Members and subscribers	96
12.2	Any other offsite users?	97
12.3	Reliability or representativeness of data on other offsite usage	101
13.	**Outreach and Non-routine Services**	102
14.	**Automation Potential**	104
14.1	Current computer access	104
14.2	Current computer usage	106
14.3	Potential usage: Desire to automate	110
15.	**Appendices**	114
15.1	Recruiting letter	115
15.2	Questionnaire	116
15.3	Bibliography	123

1. Why and How Staffing Ratios were Studied (Introduction)

1.1 Aims and scope

The general and ultimate wider aim of studies of this kind is establishment of user: "librarian" and/or information worker ratios or quotients for use in forecasting and planning at both the national and organisational level. The immediate specific aim of this study was to establish such ratios for the "special" sector of the library-information field.

1.11 *Quantitative aim*

To investigate and further define the numerical relationship of special library-information staff to actual and potential user populations – in a number of different ways and dimensions. The end result aimed at was production of staff : user ratios based on existing norms. Such ratios are frequently used to good effect by other labour-intensive service professions for manpower and systems planning purposes (both corporate and national).

1.12 *Qualitative aim*

Existing or prevailing norms are interesting and useful factual data in their own right. Yet they may represent staffing levels which are less than ideal, or even satisfactory, from the point of view of service managers and the users or persons served. For this reason it also seemed desirable to attempt some preliminary exploration of the effectiveness of various staffing levels and staff: user ratios. The aim here was to go beyond coverage of existing norms (as described in 1.11) and (in the absence of more firmly based and exhaustively researched "standards") indicate "desirable" or "satisfactory" levels which might serve as interim staffing guidelines. This kind of information may also be useful to forecasters as fairly realistic input to optimistic, relatively high demand scenarios ("best" as opposed to "worst" mode forecasts).

1.13 *Scope and range of study*

The scope of the study was restricted to the "special" sector – as defined by the Department of Education and Science Census (see section 1.3 *Methodology* for listing of service types included under this heading). Reasons for this decision were dual and inter-related. This was the sector in which least was known about normative and possibly more satisfactory alternative ratios. Yet it was an area in which real need for such information existed and was actively expressed by managers and practitioners. It was believed however, that the two other major sectors of the field (public and educational) were relatively well supplied with information. Therefore no research seemed indicated at the time of planning and writing (though review may be needed at some stage in the future).

1.2 Justification or rationale for such work

1.21 *Company or service manpower planning*

The absence of data of the type described is often deplored by individual managers of special library-information services and by organisations and employers considering the establishment of new special services.

In the absence of norms or guidelines the OECD publication "Does your firm need its own information service?" was apparently still used at the time of writing. This seems highly undesirable, as it contains obsolete data (published 1962). It does however point to a need. From time to time one hears reinforcing comments within the profession about the desirability of updating or extending the work reported on in this OECD monograph. So, a study of the kind described in this report would produce data of apparent immediate practical use to library-information managers in the special sector.

The situation of public libraries is somewhat different. Basic data on staff size and populations served has been collected and assessed by the LAMSAC team for the public sector (Staffing of public libraries: a report of the research undertaken by the Local Authorities Management Services and Computer Committee for the Department of Education and Science. 2v. London, HMSO, 1976). The educational sector also appears to possess internally produced staffing standards of its own and a collected body of data on population size and parameters.

1.22 *National manpower planning for the library-information work force as a whole*

Sufficient data bases now exist to set library-information work force planning on a systematic basis. In the light of current economic and manpower problems in the UK generally and our profession specifically, this would seem a desirable thing to do. Staff : user ratios would be extremely useful input to national manpower planning.

Recent exploratory work by the author for the BLRDD, on national manpower forecasting and planning practices in other occupations and industries, revealed that known ratios or accepted standards of worker to relevant user populations are typical and essential building blocks, in forecasting for labour-intensive service professions like librarianship or information work. (Slater,

M. Manpower forecasting and planning. *J. Inf. Sci.* 1(3) Aug. 79. pp. 131–43). Such ratios or quotients are known and used in teacher, doctor, pharmacist and other NHS staff category forecasting. Some politely restrained surprise was expressed by other forecasters interviewed, that we did not know such things about the library-information profession as a whole. The Government White Paper: "Organic change in local government" (1979) provides further evidence of other established staff : user ratios – e.g. for education, the social services, local government planners and traffic managers. It also makes estimates for libraries (public only) in terms of staff expansion. So, any attempt to shed light on existing norms and optimal levels in the special sector would complete the picture for the library-information field as a whole. This would provide material of great utility to library-information planners and forecasters at the wider national level. At the moment we lack data available to and considered vital by other comparable professions. This report represents an attempt to start or stimulate its systematic collection and dissemination.

1.23 Built-in obsolescence as an argument against a project of this type

It could be argued that our culture is now undergoing a period of such rapid technological change – and partly consequential social restructuring – that a project of this type is not justified. Will its results and ratios be obsolete before project completion and publications?

Equally valid counter-arguments exist concerning the desirability of monitoring change. Planning and predictive insights are gained by before and after studies. The term before and after however, implies a finite period of transition or change. The real world seldom works in this way. Change is a long term ongoing process and transition a continuous state of the environmental flux.

In the light of these comments the obsolescence theory seemed a valid cautionary influence on the nature and scope of work undertaken, rather than complete deterrent. There seems in fact a case for setting up a programme of individual short-term temperature taking exercises over a period of time. This would be dependent on updating policies for existing data in the other major sectors. In the light of current external context, a massive long-term one-off study, aiming to "settle this issue once and for all" and amassing data for a period of years before reporting, seemed unproductive, unjustified and frankly ridiculous.

What was recommended instead was an initial fairly short-term project of a 6 man-months duration. Advantages of this approach included: reporting back fairly quickly on the status quo; exploration of the possibility and utility of further research without initially committing too much in the way of funds or manpower.

To sum up: there seemed little merit in a massive, pseudodefinitive, never to be repeated study, when results might be rapidly superseded. But there did seem to be a genuine case for exploring the possibility of setting up a monitoring system to check on existing and optimal staffing levels and user ratios at repeated intervals. This might be at regular or irregular intervals but would continue over time. The project reported here could act as an exploratory pilot or feasibility study for such an extended exercise as well as producing immediately useful, if time-dependent, data in its own right.

1.3 Methodology and detailed aims

1.31 Instruments

Mass data seemed necessary to provide reliable ratios and reveal meaningful trends. This rather inevitably dictated the use of a fairly large sample of units and a self-completed, mail distributed and returned questionnaire or form as the data gathering method.

Such a methodology did not however preclude simultaneous exploration of the qualitative aspects and implications of various staffing levels and policies and various staff to user ratios encountered, via a mix of factual and open-ended or more speculative questions. The former provided information on normative ratios, the latter on optimum, ideal, or better ratios. To give a crude example, one can ask about existing staff levels, and about actual demand, traffic, user numbers, and the size of the population that might theoretically be served. This sort of question provides existing ratio data. One can also ask how satisfactory current staffing levels were felt to be and in what dimensions (number and/or qualifications, experience, motivation, etc.). One can even ask for quantification of such belief – what size of staff would the librarian need to run the service "properly" or at optimum level.

This kind of question can lead to tentative "optimal" ratios for present conditions. If one wanted to get projective information one could build in various options or parameters – like expansion of the service in ways the librarian considered desirable in the future. But I felt that at this stage this was undesirable (too hypothetical, anticipated forecasting on an amateurish level, added to the size of the research project). One could however ask about use of or access to terminals within the organisation. Using this information, one might draw some conclusions about potential for mechanisation, which would affect staffing levels of the future.

1.32 Sample

Blanket distribution of the questionnaire to most special services in the DES Census listing was adopted (2,100 valid addresses of units were used). Response rate in the library-information field being variable and unpredictable, this seemed advisable strategy to ensure adequate size of received sample. (Response rate achieved by this survey was 31%, 655 units.) The special sector itself is sub-divided into services of differing kinds which one would wish to analyse and consider separately. Sub-categories of the special field, or units, included in the sample comprise: industrial and commercial; local government (other than public library); government department, station or agency; public corporation; learned or professional society; research or trade association (Census code categories 6, 7, 9, 10, 11, 12). A copy of the questionnaire used is provided as an appendix (Section 15.2).

1.33   *Definition of terms and parameters*

The major end-product of the study was a variety of ratios or quotients (both actual and where relevant "optimal"), such as:

  – staff: actual user
  – staff: potential user
  – staff: total theoretically relevant population*

Having actually obtained these different ratios, it should be possible to see more clearly which of them is most meaningful and useable for planning purposes either corporate or national. But to produce these ratios it was necessary to define carefully what was meant by each of the terms employed. This was not an easy task.

What was meant for instance by the word "staff"? Should it be restricted to qualified staff? If so, how was "qualified" defined? Did it include people only possessing other (non library-information) degrees and diplomas? Did it include qualified by experience – i.e. the "semi-professional"? Should "staff" include non-professional, or even the larger category of support staff? As we were (and are) planning for a profession some restriction would appear to be necessary, but needed to be carefully decided upon. All these questions arising required consideration before the ratios presented in this report could be produced. Similar questions had to be asked and answered about definitions of actual user, potential user, total relevant population. Particular difficulties existed in the special sector in defining the relevant populations on the user side of the ratio.

The existence of both onsite and offsite user populations further complicated the issue. It would seem that in many special services the onsite user population is just the tip of the iceberg. Membership organisations are a typical example of this phenomenon, but it also occurs in other less expected contexts. Of course, the further offsite the user population gets, the softer and less reliable any numerical "data" concerning its size and actual usage habits becomes!

---

* Usually, but by no means necessarily, total number of employees of an organisation, etc. Membership organisations for example and some "learned" special libraries have a far wider definition of this category.

2. Summary

2.1 Published statistics as a ratio source

Published data on staff to user ratios in the special library–information field is lacking. Obviously so, otherwise there would have been little point in producing this report. Separately published official sources however exist which do record: the size and structure of the library–information population; general UK population and employment statistics from which one might be able to construct or deduce potential user groups.

Theoretically, one ought to be able to use these two data sets in combination, to produce generalised ratios reflecting the status quo. Various problems of data incompatibility sometimes obstruct exercises of this kind. The obvious candidate for library-information population data was the Department of Education and Science: Census of staff in librarianship and information work in the United Kingdom 1976. (HMSO, 1978). So a wider-based statistical publication had to be sought which was compatible in time of data collection and in other ways (e.g. classification of manpower as qualified and unqualified) with the DES Library Census. One reliable and reputable publication met these demands neatly. It was: *Lindley*, R. (ed.) Britain's medium-term employment prospects. Warwick University, Manpower Research Group 1978.

Generalised ratios derived from comparison of the two data sets are provided in section 3 of the main report. They indicate that library-information workers in general and special librarians and information personnel in particular are spread fairly thin as far as their potential users in the entire UK population are concerned. Numbers on the user side of the ratios are rather higher than those pertaining in other service professions which might be considered comparable. The doctor to potential patient ratio for instance is 1:820. The social worker ratio is 7·5 per 1,000 population, or 1:133. The ideal teacher: pupil ratio is 1:30, the actuality in 1979 was approaching this at 1:33.

Ratios for the library-information field depend on how one defines library-information worker and potential user. If for instance, one takes *qualified special* library-information workers (the most relevant definition within the terms of this report) and sets their total number against that of the qualified labour force, narrowly defined (excluding skilled trades), one comes up with a ratio of 1:970. If one takes *all special* library-information workers (regardless of qualification or grade-level) and sets them against a wider definition of potential user – i.e. the qualified employed broadly defined – one comes up with a ratio of 1:1466. Both ratios are indicative of relative scarcity of special library-information workers to serve the potential user population.

Strictly speaking, they are more indicative of a scarcity of libraries and information units or uneven distribution of library-information expertise. In actuality we have a patchy or pocketed spread, because some organisations provide library-information units at the work-place as an aid to employees, whereas others do not. Astute readers will notice that some ratios derived from published sources give a more "favourable" and manageable impression of potential user populations than survey-derived ratios. Overlap of user populations of actual services is the probable cause (plus difficulty in estimating offsite populations?). This discrepancy underlines the dangers of reliance on a single source of ratio data. (See section 3 for published statistics.)

2.2 Ratios emerging directly from this study

Survey data, on which ratios constructed for this report were based, represents fairly reliable "of the order of" material. Extent of "fuzzy answer" (estimate or guess) is known. "Clear" or absolutely correct data on inhouse potential users were supplied by 70% of the sample, approximations (rounded figures) by 11%, estimates by 14%, and guesses by 5%. Answers on total payroll complement of participating organisations reached an even better degree of accuracy, with only 11% estimates and 2% guess answers. This in itself may be the first indication of a point that will be returned to later. Perhaps insufficient attention is given by some special library-information managers to the definition and assessment of their potential users within the organisation.

Taking this trend into consideration and in the complete absence of ratios based on more exhaustive study, data provided by respondents was felt to be useable material from which to derive tentative ratios which may be useful as staffing guidelines or attrition defences. This claim holds up well in the onsite user context, it may be more debatable in the offsite user context.

Ratios are provided on various levels, using different definitions of both user and of library-information staff. A distinction is made between onsite or direct responsibility and offsite user populations. The membership institution is a recognised anomaly in this context. Actual, potential and theoretically possible user populations are also considered.

On the library-information staff side, a distinction is made between qualified staff and total staff (including the unqualified). Ratios are presented setting these staff distinctions against the various definitions of user group.

Normative and optimal or "ideal" ratios are also provided. Ratios reflecting the status quo are given, but it was realised that their use as staffing guidelines might possibly perpetuate an undesirable staffing level. So respondents were also asked to specify staffing levels needed to run the present service properly without stress; to expand and improve it. These questions were responsibly and thoughtfully answered. Some respondents, for instance, said that they could manage with fewer staff.

Some library-information managers seemed to prefer workload analysis to user ratios as a staffing requirements measure. So actual traffic or workload ratios are also provided. These are based on records of a test day.

For the sample as a whole, the actual ratios just described were as follows:

Normative for onsite user population:

1 special-library information worker (of any kind) to 56 actual onsite users, 135 potential onsite users, 267 theoretically possible onsite users.

1 professionally qualified* library-information worker to 194 actual onsite users, 469 potential onsite users, 927 theoretically possible onsite users.

Normative ratios including offsite users:

1 special library-information worker (of any kind) to 284 actual onsite and offsite users and 4,820 potential onsite and offsite users (when one comes to consider offsite populations it is impossible to define a "theoretically possible" population).

1 qualified special library-information worker to 984 actual onsite and offsite users and 16,709 potential onsite and offsite users.

Ideal ratios to run present type of service properly and comfortably for onsite users:

1 special library-information worker (of any kind) to 50 actual onsite users, 121 potential onsite users, 240 theoretically possible onsite users.

Ideal ratio to run present service properly for onsite plus offsite user population:

1 special library-information worker (of any kind) to 254 actual onsite and offsite users, 4321 potential onsite and offsite users.

Ideal ratios allowing for expansion of service in desirable directions, onsite users only:

1 special library-information worker (of any kind) to 43 actual onsite users, 103 potential onsite users, 204 theoretically possible onsite users.

---

*The actual DES Census definition was "staff occupying post for qualified librarian or information" ... Unfortunately this is slightly at variance with the definition used elsewhere in the report.

Ideal ratios for expansion, onsite plus offsite users:

1 special library-information worker (of any kind) to 217 actual onsite and offsite users, 3686 potential onsite and offsite users.

Workload ratios recorded for the sample as a whole on the test day were: 1 library-information worker (of any kind) to 6·31 enquiries and 5 loans.

(See section 4 of main report for full ratio tables).

2.3 Services and their titles: What's in a name?

This study of 655 units was confined to the "special field", within which we distinguished between three kinds of special service: industry-commerce (or private, profit-making) 277 (42%); government, central and local 242 (37%); societies and associations 136 (21%). Geographical distribution of the sample was as follows: 22% were located in the North; 13% in the Midlands; 65% in the South of England.

Co-operating services were also categorised by size of parent organisation, size distribution being: minute 16%; small 23%; medium 34%; large 22%; unknown 4%. *(For numerical definition of these size categories please see section 5.1).*

Service title and service function (the latter as perceived by the unit head) seemed important pieces of information to acquire. When cross-analysed, variation in extent of correlation between title and function became evident. The title "library" accurately described function in only 31% of cases. The majority of head "librarians" felt that what their unit really did could better be described as a "combined library-information service". The same was true of the formal title "Information" (unit, department, service): 29% of heads felt that this was an accurate description; 54% thought that what they were really operating was again a combined library-information service; 17% felt that both information and/or library were misleading descriptions and that their service should have some different name. Services officially called combined thought that this accurately described their function in 91% of cases. Services possessing some "different" title were pleased by its appropriateness in 76% of cases.

The moral of these findings seems clear. More care generally needs to be taken in the specific naming of individual library-information services. The titles library or information service, alone and unqualified, would both seem to be suspect. Higher management (if you ever read this) please take note. Please do not call it the library or the information service, unless you are sure that is what it really is – and the unit head agrees with you.

The title indicated by our findings, preferred as descriptive of the real nature of most current work, would seem to be a combined one – e.g. Library-Information Unit; Technical Library and Information Department (or vice versa); Information and Library Services, etc. A title that will also please unit heads who do have some organisational function or responsibility other than library-information work, is a title that is completely or partially different, describing or implying this different responsibility, duty or expertise – e.g. Information and Publications; Library and Editorial Services; Educational Services and Documentation; Public Relations and Information; Statistics and Market Intelligence Department.

Such preferences matter and an accurate, yet evocatively descriptive title is important. It conditions user expectations, usage levels and satisfaction levels. It may well even affect user identification and location of potentially useful services (i.e. use and non-use). If a service is called "The Library" or "The Information Department" it may be ignored and by-passed by the seeker after statistical data. But if it is called "Statistics and Market Intelligence", this person probably will find it and be happy with the result. Provided, of course, that the service really does live up to its title.

Within the profession we are always talking about ways to publicise the service. Often this seems easier to discuss than do. An absolutely correct and yet invitingly worded title (honest but user friendly), is an obvious form of basic self-publicity. Yet it would seem to have been badly neglected. On this subject of service title definition, there seems room for discussion between higher management and library-information management. An additional and useful spin-off result of such conference might be further and sharper definition of unit function within the organisation. Ultimately this should reduce both library-information worker alienation, and false "user expectations" at higher management levels.

(For more information about participating units and sample structure, see section 5, the Services).

2.4 Staffing structures

Average staff size of special library-information units amongst our sample was 5·2 people. This represents total library-information staff complement – i.e. all grades and posts included. Within this total, the average composition or staff structure was as follows:

    2·2   professional jobs:
    1·5   semi-professional jobs;
    1·5   support jobs;

So, the average special unit in our sample was a small and top-heavy structure. Incidentally, the professional jobs mentioned above may or may not be filled by professionally or otherwise qualified people. In fact, the same is true of the other two categories, semi-professional and support.

Concerning qualifications, averages per unit were: 2·4 people with some kind of qualification acquired via higher education (1·5 of these being library-information ones), 2·8 people with no qualifications at all. Some variation occurred between the different kinds of special service – e.g. both industry-commerce and societies-associations seemed to have proportionally fewer unqualified people on the staff than did government services. *For full details the reader is referred to Table 27, section 6.*

This table should be consulted carefully, always with reference to the initial "staff total" column. A large number of unqualified staff *may* just reflect a typically larger service all-round rather than a service weighted towards lack of qualification.

Indications of possible mismatch between posts and qualifications may already have been noted by astute readers. Their suspicions seem justified by our evidence.

18% of participating services had no qualified people on the staff at all – and this is defining qualification very broadly. It does not mean that there were no qualified librarians or information scientists. It means these services were entirely staffed by totally unqualified people.

16% of services had no professionally qualified library-information workers, although some staff members had other (i.e. subject or irrelevant) degrees or qualifications.

31% of services had only library-information qualifications represented in staff expertise.

35% had a mixture of library-information and other qualifications.

Please note that the last three categories above do not imply that everybody on the staff was so qualified. Only one member of staff may be involved.

Mismatch between posts and qualifications seems implicit in the above findings. This issue of mismatch was specifically examined (*see also* section 6.2 Table 32) and the following results emerged. In 23% of services there was total mismatch of posts and qualifications (everybody on the staff seemed to be "in the wrong job" at least as far as formal qualification or its lack was concerned). In 41% of services some degree of mismatch could be observed. In 36% of services there was no obvious mismatch. Mismatch was more prevalent in small and medium-sized organisations, in industry, in services called "information" or something "different", and in non-medical services.

These findings indicate an important possibility. More jobs for emergent library–school leavers and for mature unemployed qualified library-information workers may exist than was suspected. Hidden within the workforce, these posts are currently occupied by unqualified people. Distinct possibilities for "taking up slack" may exist here, but need to be carefully explored. In specific cases, the unqualified may actually be performing these jobs very well indeed. In the real work experience and aptitude are often better qualifications than pieces of paper or letters after the name. Natural wastage and the mobility of a fairly "nomadic profession" would however seem to afford employers some scope for internal re-structuring of the workforce. Whenever unqualified "librarians" leave or retire, the employer should be urged to replace with qualified personnel. To make unqualified "librarians" redundant would be unjust and difficult within the law. It is however also unjust that jobs within the profession should be occupied by the unqualified, while some qualified remain unemployed (or otherwise employed) without. A situation that needs rectification exists here, but needs to be handled with the utmost management sensitivity and skill and above all humanely.

The question of part-time employment was also examined. If our sample is typical, it would seem that the normal structure of the special service is "full-time workers only". This was the case in 71% of units, 19% employed part-timers as well as full-timers, and 10% ran on part-time staffing only. *(See section 6 for further information on staffing structures).*

2.5 Doomwatch scenario: A shrinking profession?

Sixteen percent of services in our sample were carrying frozen posts at the time of our survey (late 1979). Average number of frozen posts per unit was: in units with frozen posts 1·54; amongst the sample as a whole 0·25.

The number of frozen posts at any given point in time does not necessarily correlate perfectly with whether, over time and as a matter of policy, the service is growing or shrinking. During the year prior to our survey, 13% of participating services had grown in staff size, 76% had remained the same, 11% had shrunk. This indicates that some of the frozen posts (reportedly carried by 16% of the sample) were of long duration. *(See section 7 for more information).*

2.6 Staffing adequacy: Size and composition

Understaffing in numerical terms was reported by 44% of respondents. When asked to specify the level of staffing really necessary, the average unit seemed to need a part-timer in addition to the existing complement, in order to maintain current service properly and without stress. To expand or improve the service, the average unit would seem to need another full-time member of staff (as well as the part-timer). *(For full details and variations between sub-groups of the sample, readers should consult section 8, Table 39).*

Staff quality seemed to give less cause for concern or worry than staff quantity. Only 15% of services were suffering from really poor staff performance. Opinions about the reasons for poor performance were sought. According to our sample, factors affecting performance are subjectively slanted, rather than matters of objective fact. Qualification, experience and training were not the major influential factors as far as inefficiency or unsuitability were concerned.

The most frequently cited single cause was context-induced low morale (mentioned by 47%). This lays the blame for poor staff performance squarely at the employer's feet. Matters of pay, conditions of work, career and promotion prospects (or their lack) and general low status within the organisation were raised as evidence.

Two other major causes of inefficiency were given. Lack of interest and basic motivation on the employee's part was mentioned by 44%. This factor may be causally related to work-environment induced low morale. The wrong personality for the occupation or the specific post was cited by 37%. *(For full details and subsidiary causes see section 8, Table 41).*

2.7 Current ways of assessing staffing levels

Methods in current use were not found to be really satisfactory in practice in most cases. Only 14% of respondents approved, or whole-heartedly supported them. Why was this? Partly the methods themselves were thought to be intrinsically at fault and partly it seemed a matter of how they were applied.

The head of the library-information unit did not seem to have enough say in the process. In 35% of cases, central management or imported "outside experts" made assessments and all decisions arising. In 16% of cases the unit head's opinion was not sought and s/he was not consulted, or even properly informed about rationale for decisions or methods by which they were reached. In 31% of units in our sample there was allegedly no real systematic assessment of staffing requirements or any logical decision-making. Either the service "just grew like topsy" (15%), or hopefully educated guesswork based on past experience was relied on (16%). Financial and economic pressures were the real deciding factors, according to 25% of the sample: "Not what we need, but what we can afford".

More positive approaches included workload analysis (24%), demand related staffing (22%), forward planning and service provision related staffing (19%), and research and/or statistics based methods (9%). Methods were not necessarily mutually exclusive. Usage of more than one method was quite common. Only 5% were using staff to user ratios and 3% were using ratios other than staff to user – e.g. workload based, departmental or subject area ratios.

Reactions to the idea of staff to user ratio methodology stressed the practical difficulties of assessing the size of either the potential or the actual user group. Some respondents felt that potential user group size was a poor predictor of actual usage. Others maintained that actual user numbers did not necessarily correlate with actual usage volume. Fluctuating demand from a fairly static user population was cited. Isolate the factors causing such fluctuation, these respondents believed, and you may find a real predictive measure or assessment tool.

(For more information on assessment methodology see section 9).

2.8 User populations

Taking up the issue raised by respondents concerning existence of correlation between actual, potential and theoretically possible user populations, we re-examined the ratios and the raw data on which they were based. This exercise proved worthwhile. Some consistent trends or relationships did show up, but only in the onsite or inhouse section.

Potential onsite users tended to represent roughly half the total payroll. Actual users represented about 40% of the potential population, or 20% of the total payroll (or total theoretically possible user population). Obviously there was some variation amongst the sub-groups of the sample, but it was clustered around these average percentages. *(See also section 10.1, Table 46).*

User populations were also divided into onsite and offsite. The large majority of services (73%) catered for a thoroughly mixed onsite and offsite user population. Only 15% of services catered almost exclusively for the more predictable onsite user. Eighty-six percent of the sample had some outside users (other than members). Eighteen percent had an official membership or body of subscribers to be serviced. Outside users other than members included bona fide users, the general public, ex-employees, teachers and pupils, organisations in the same line of business and other librarians and information officers *(See section 12.2, Tables 60–61).*

The percentage of actual use arising from the offsite potential population was far smaller than that observed in the onsite population. More variation also occurred between industry-commerce, government and society services in percentage of actual use by offsite population. *(See section 10.2, Tables 48–9).*

So offsite usage was a common phenomenon, although usage levels were allegedly below onsite ones – in more than one sense (frequency and volume of use per individual user and actual users as a percentage of potential). Probably this is merciful, because the offsite groups involved were very large. For librarians with a strong commitment to help the public or the bona fide user, the sheer size of these groups could be seen as a potential threat to system stability. This is why some unit heads fear publicising the service or attempting to convert the non-user. "Dont stir up a demand we can't meet". Offsite users present the library-information manager with major problems of handling and prediction. Higher management should acquaint itself, sympathetically, with this problem. It is just possible that too much outside use is made of special libraries and information units – particularly industrial-commercial ones. Higher management might decide however that such usage was justified. A good case, on public relations and profitability grounds, can be made for help given to doctors, dentists, veterinarians and pharmacists by library-information units in the pharmaceutical industry. Many other profit-making organisations may also be able to justify information supply to customers, clients and contractors. If this were officially sanctioned policy, however, most library-information units affected would need more staff. The problem and its solution should not be left for the unit head to cope with, from existing resources. That is expecting the impossible. Any compromising solutions reached at that level can only be made at the expense of the library-information staff and the onsite user.

Our attempt to establish offsite user ratios was ultimately I feel an informative failure. The populations concerned are often so large that they are unguessable by the unit head and they may change over time. But the very reason for failure to achieve objective has exposed what may be a much more important issue. It has ventilated the offsite usage predicament facing the majority of special library-information workers. Onsite usage, for which we can establish ratios, would seem to be only the tip of the user iceberg.

Onsite usage itself revealed another problem of a different kind. Evidence emerged indicating that the potential onsite user may be insufficiently defined – particularly in view of general understaffing problems. Open-house policies towards onsite usage (anyone and everyone welcomed) were adopted by 31% of our sample, 25% had loosely defined potential user groups or a fairly free and easy access policy, 44% had tightly defined potential user policies. This last mentioned group had "thought it all through" and knew exactly who their users ought to be in terms of organisational aims.

Priority groups (in the services which had priorities) were: important people – the decision-makers, regardless of subject discipline or orientation; subject specialists in fields relevant to the organisation's function – e.g. engineers, scientists, doctors – this could however be at any level – e.g. 27% included technicians in their priority "in-group".

Commercial, financial, marketing and publicising functions tended to be low in priority. The technical side and the policy makers were the people given priority service in the typical special unit which *has* sorted out its priorities. *(For full details the reader is referred to sections 10, 11, 12. Section 10 provides a general discussion of user definition, section 11 examines onsite usage and section 12 offsite usage).*

2.9 Personpower alternatives: automation potential

Basically, the subject of this report lies within the discipline of manpower planning. Currently that wider field is much exercised by questions concerning the impact of new technology, its effect on the labour-force and on the user or consumer of services and products.

This being the case, it seemed relevant to examine mechanisation potential and actuality in the special library-information field.

Scope for mechanised extension of service provision did appear to exist. Ninety-one percent of our sample indulged in what might be described as "out-reach" provision or active, outgoing services to users, either manual, or machine-aided. What was provided however tended to be fairly basic familiar stuff – e.g. journal circulation (71%), current awareness (67%), SDI (55%). *(See section 13 Outreach and non-routine services).*

Actual involvement in mechanisation was currently heavy but relatively recent. Forty-six percent of the sample had mechanised some part of their service and/or were doing on-line searches. A further 12% were planning to do so. Forty-two percent had no plans to mechanise. Only 32% had no current access to computers or terminals.

Involvement appeared to have been a recent occurrence in most cases. Average time operational was 3½ years (mean average). The range was from a few months to 18 years. Only 6 services however reported a system that had been operational for longer than 10 years.

Main usage was for searching: 30% of the whole sample were conducting mechanised searches, either on-line or batch. External commercial data bases were used by 25%. Here BLAISE lead, mentioned by 74 respondents. Its only real competitors were Lockheed DIALOG (56 mentions) and DIAL-TECH (30 mentions).

Creation of own data bases was mentioned by 13%, computerised cataloguing by 11%, computer produced publications and services to users (SDI etc) were mentioned by 12%. ONly 2% were doing really novel or experimental work – e.g. full text retrieval, programmed learning as part of user education. *(See section 14, Automation Potential for more information)*.

Note: This is a long summary, prepared partly as a self-contained alternative to the main report for the generalist casual reader, partly as a synoptic guide to contents and major findings for the committed reader with a practical use for findings. If you fall into the latter category don't stop here. You will find much more specific material and further recommendations in the ensuing text. So, if applicable (and I rather hope it is), now please read on . . .

3. Any Relevant Data Publicly Available?

The Department of Education and Science Census of library-information staff exists in published form, and so do various official or officially approved analyses of the whole population of the United Kingdom. These represent two sources of information which, if combined, might provide general data or ratios of the type used for planning purposes by some other professions.

Typical examples, drawn from the Government White Paper on Organic Change (1979) include: "London Boroughs, with average population of 213,000 have a ratio of 7·50" social services workers per 1,000 population; "The metropolitan districts have an average population of 321,000 and staff ratio of 30·28" teachers per 1,000 population.

It would be argued that comparable figures for our profession might have little relevance to potential usage and even less to actual usage patterns. Perhaps this is particularly true of the special library-information field, with which this report is specifically concerned. But as a brief piece of desk research, setting us in a broader context (as many other service occupations do set themselves for planning purposes) it may be worthwhile to examine what is available relevant to our field. (Even if it only demonstrates the inapplicability of this mode of thought to the special library-information scene, and the greater suitability for planning purposes of user ratios obtained direct from operating services.)

We are set in a rather different situation from that of many other service professions. Most people need the health services of pharmacist, dentist and doctor at some time or another in their lives. The Health Service originally intended these services to be equally and relatively inexpensively available to all needing them. Education is a service compulsory on us by law (up to a certain age, which can vary over the decades). Nobody however, is forced in any sense to use libraries or information services. Nor are library-information services necessarily available at the workplace for those who do feel a need for such work-aids. These services may not be provided at all, or they may be provided only for certain categories of employee.

Nevertheless, it may be of interest to readers to see the results of a quick broad scale scan of some published data. The DES Census was the obvious choice for the library-information population data. Which source to use for the general UK population and workforce statistics did present problems of choice. The decision to use "Britain's medium-term employment prospects" (Manpower Research Group, Warwick University. Editor: Robert Lindley) was based on several factors. The data this publication contains is directly comparable in time-setting with the DES Census. Both publications present figures collected in 1976 and published in 1978. So there was no danger of error or discrepancy caused purely by time-lag (or comparing the temporally incomparable). The mode in which the data was viewed and analysed by Lindley et al was also highly suitable. It was intended (like the DES Census) for use in manpower forecasting and planning.

The following ratios resulted from comparison of the two sets of statistics (DES and Warwick). Minimum verbal category descriptors were used in this listing, for the sake of clear layout and ease of assimilation. Base figures shown to the right of each category descriptor represent numbers of people involved.

Notes following the listing should clarify any ambiguous descriptors for readers in doubt about meaning or coverage.

Ratios derived from published data

Table 1

		Base	Ratio
All library-information workers[1] (Public, Educational and Special) versus whole UK population			
(a) All library-information workers, all grades		44604	
vs.			1 : 1220
Whole UK population (minus library-information workers)		54427396	
(b) All qualified[2] library-information workers		17259	
vs.			1 : 3154
Whole UK population (minus library-information workers)[3]		54427396	

19

Table 2

All library-information workers (PE & S) versus the UK labour force[4]

		Base	Ratio
(a)	All library-information workers, all grades	44604	
	vs.		1 : 576
	UK Labour force (minus library-information workers)	25680396	
(b)	All qualified library-information workers	17259	
	vs.		1 : 1488
	UK Labour force (minus library-information workers)	25680396	

Table 3

All library-information workers (PE & S) versus UK employed population

		Base	Ratio
(a)	All library-information workers, all grades	44604	
	vs.		1 : 538
	UK employed population (minus library-information workers)	24003396	
(b)	All qualified library-information workers	17259	
	vs.		1 : 1391
	UK employed population (minus library-information workers)	24003396	

Table 4

Public library staff versus whole UK population	Base	Ratio
(a) Public and national library staff, all grades	28120	
vs.		1 : 1936
Whole UK population (minus public library staff)[3]	54443880	
(b) Qualified public and national library staff	9098	
vs.		1 : 5984
Whole UK population (minus public library staff)	54443880	

Table 5

Academic library-information staff versus students in non-compulsory education[5]	Base	Ratio
(a) "Academic" library-information staff, all grades	8270	
vs.		1 : 947
People (over 16) in non-compulsory education	7834000	
(b) Qualified library-information staff	3989	
vs.		1 : 1964
People (over 16) in non-compulsory education	7834000	

Table 6

Special library-information staff versus UK labour force

		Base	Ratio
(a)	Special library-information staff, all grades	9447	
	vs.		1 : 2718
	UK labour force (minus all library-information workers)	25680396	
(b)	Qualified special library-information staff	4367	
	vs.		1 : 5881
	UK labour force (minus all library-information workers)	25680396	

Table 7

Special library-information staff versus UK employed population

		Base	Ratio
(a)	Special library-information staff, all grades	9447	
	vs.		1 : 2541
	UK employed population (minus all library-information workers)	24003396	
(b)	Qualified special library-information staff	4367	
	vs.		1 : 5496
	UK employed population (minus all library-information workers)	24003396	

Table 8

Special library-information staff versus
UK qualified[6] labour force

		Base	Ratio
(a)	Special library-information staff, all grades	9447	
	vs.		1 : 1505
	Qualified labour force, broadly defined (including skilled manual and "other non-manual").	14222000	
(b)	Qualified special library-information staff	4367	
	vs.		1 : 3257
	Qualified labour force, broadly defined	14222000	
(c)	Special library-information staff, all grades	9447	
	vs.		1 : 449
	Qualified labour force, narrowly defined (excluding skilled manual and "other non-manual")	4237000	
(d)	Qualified special library-information staff	4367	
	vs.		1 : 970
	Qualified labour force, narrowly defined	4237000	

Table 9

Special library-information staff versus UK qualified[6] employed

		Base	Ratio
(a)	Special library-information staff, all grades	9447	
	vs.		1 : 1466
	Qualified employed, broadly defined.	13847000	
(b)	Qualified special library-information staff	4367	
	vs.		1 : 3171
	Qualified employed, broadly defined	13847000	
(c)	Special library-information staff, all grades	9447	
	vs.		1 : 443
	Qualified employed, narrowly defined	4186000	
(d)	Qualified special library-information staff	4367	
	vs.		1 : 959
	Qualified employed, narrowly defined	4186000	

Explanatory notes to Tables 1 to 9

[1] *Use of the term "library-information worker" in various contexts:* No distinction is made between librarians and information workers in this ratio "table". In all cases the employed sector is the base. (Census data was derived from organisations, not individuals and so could not include the unemployed). This is also a "full-time equivalent" count, post-based rather than head-count. The actual number of employed library-information workers, counting each part-timer as a single unit, rather than as a FTE contributory unit, would obviously make the library-information workforce somewhat larger. It would also make the potential user appear to be better served than s/he actually is, so the "full-time equivalent" approach was chosen.

[2] *"Qualified" library-information worker*: the actual DES Census definition was "staff occupying post for qualified librarian or information scientist". Admittedly this is a bit different. Apologies for any misleading implications of the necessarily shorthand descriptor.

[3] *"Minus library-information workers"*: wherever possible, the library-information workforce (or the relevant segment of it) was subtracted from the larger potential user population (which in official statistics would obviously include it). The rationale in the case of public library ratios, for only subtracting the public "librarians" is that other kinds of librarians and information workers are potential public library users.

[4] *United Kingdom Labour Force* : The term "labour force" includes inactive stock – ie. those unemployed but actively seeking or desiring work are included. This contrasts with the UK employed population (actively and gainfully employed) with which it should not be confused.

[5] *"Academic" library-information staff and their potential users* : Although the term "academic" was used the category is broader, including such tertiary educational institutions as polytechnics, technical colleges, etc. It does not include school libraries or school children (primary or secondary) as potential users. Neither does it include institutions like "6th form colleges" where secondary education is pursued in an alternative setting. The potential user group is defined as people over 16 undergoing non-compulsory education (of a tertiary nature).

Unfortunately it does not include "academic" teaching staff in the potential user population. This proved impossible to assess, because the Warwick occupational classification did not distinguish between school teachers and tertiary education establishment teaching staff.

[6] *Qualified labour force and employed sector* : It would have been consistent and desirable to subtract the special library-information sector from the qualified labour force (where necessary), as was done in some other sections of our listing table. This proved impossible, for several reasons: uncertainty about how, where (or even if) Warwick distinguished between professional and support staff in the library-information field; where Warwick classified library-information work under its broad band headings; whether Warwick distinguished between librarianship and information work and classified them – admittedly under some other blanket heading(s) – together or apart. To ask some illustrative questions:

Would library support staff and semi-professionals be classed by Warwick as "clerical" or as "other non-manual"?

Would librarians come under "other professions" and information scientists, under "scientists, technologists and engineers"? Or would both go under "other professions"? Would academic librarians be separately classed under "education professions"? In the face of this type of problem it seemed safer to attempt no subtraction. In any case special librarians and information workers represent a small fragment of the whole qualified sector. So perhaps our inability to subtract them is not too disastrous or error-productive. As additional justification for non-subtraction, I could perhaps add that there is evidence from our survey that special library-information workers are one another's users. This happens via formal and informal library-information networks. (*See also* main body of report, section 12.2).

The qualified labour force (and its employed sector) is divided in an apparently curious way into two segments called "broadly defined" and "narrowly defined". This separation is not one used by Warwick, but one which I imposed by further clumping of Warwick's broad occupational categories.

Definitions and parameters of potential user groups supplied by respondents in our survey suggested this division. Some heads of library-information services regard anyone in a skilled occupation (other than secretarial-clerical) as a potential user. Others did not. The group we have created called "broadly defined" includes the categories "other non-manual occupation" and "skilled manual". The narrowly defined group excludes these two categories. As defined by Warwick, the group called "other non-manual" includes such occupations as: "inspectors (transport); traffic controllers; communications operators; civil service executive officers; salesmen; security workers; restaurateurs; publicans; managers of small enterprises; artists; trade union officials; laboratory assistants".

The other group "skilled occupations" includes: "all skilled workers in engineering ... and foremen", plus such jobs as woodworkers, drivers, potters, jewellers, bakers, brewers, printers, painters and decorators, construction workers. That listing is not actually exhaustive. But the reader may be exhausted and by now has probably got the general idea.

A table showing the Warwick categories (with figures) used in our "qualified" sector is provided below for those interested.

Table 10 Qualified UK labour force (broadly and narrowly defined)[1] and employed sector (thousands)[2]

	Qualified labour force	Qualified employed sector
Total	14222 (100%)	13847 (100%)
Administrators and managers	1090 (8%)	1075 (8%)
Scientists, technologists & engineers	479 (3%)	472 (3%)
Education professions	842 (6%)	836 (6%)
Health and social service	896 (6%)	890 (6%)
Other professions	520 (4%)	511 (4%)
Technicians and draughtsmen	410 (3%)	402 (3%)
Other non-manual[1]	3931 (28%)	3841 (28%)
Skilled manual[1]	6054 (42%)	5820 (42%)

[1]Occupational categories above the line represents the "qualified (fairly) narrowly defined" sector. Occupations below the line should be added to form the group "qualified broadly defined".
[2]For clarity of comparison all absolute figures have been reduced and represent thousands.

4. Ratios: Data and Comment

The hard core of the findings of this study are presented here in the compacted form of data tables. As readers will (hopefully) want to use this section as a ready-reference tool, textual comment has been kept to a minimum. The data was obtained from 655 special library-information units late in 1979. For a detailed description of the internal composition of this sample see Section 5, "The Services". In obtaining the raw data for ratio construction, an attempt was made to acquire more than just normative or status quo reflecting information. Respondents were not just asked about current library-information staffing levels. They were also asked what number of staff they would need to operate the present service properly, and what number they would need to extend or expand the service in ways they considered desirable. These questions were reasonably and realistically answered. Demands were modestly based in what would seem to be reality, not wish-fulfilment dreamland. To summarise them, on average for the sample as a whole: one part-timer more on the staff would enable the average present kind of service to operate efficiently and without stress. One more full-timer (in addition to the part-timer) would comfortably allow for expansion of service in what seem desirable directions to the person in charge. So this section is subdivided into sectors considering separately the normative ratios and what have been called (largely for want of a better word) the "ideal" ones. A third sector of ratios considers the staff to workload question. Indicative information on workload (as represented by enquiries and borrowings on a test day) was collected. Some respondents felt strongly that workload analysis was a better way of assessing staffing requirements than using staff to user ratios. So our "workload" figures are presented here, in ratio form, accompanying the other major ratio data.

In the sub-sections concerned with staff to user relationships, readers should be alerted in advance that the staff data is alternatively set against hard core and offsite user populations. Hard core represents the direct responsibility user group, onsite except in the case of membership societies or associations. Offsite includes bona fide users, "other branches of the firm", etc.

4.1 Normative staff to user ratios

Table 11 Hard core ratios for onsite or direct responsibility population

	One library-information worker[2] to...		
	Actual users	Potential users	Total onsite payroll
Whole sample–staff only	56	135	267
– plus members[1]	93	172	304
Area			
North	50	100	195
Midlands	76	160	584
South	56	145	253
Type			
Industry, Commerce	57	124	311
Government, etc.	71	181	313
Society–staff only	19	38	69
– plus members[1]	203	12784	12814
Service title			
Library[3]	78	207	403
Information[3]	12	31	52
Combined	60	118	246
Different[3]	17	35	83
Medical v. rest			
Medical	192	393	757
Non-medical	40	104	208

[1] The membership of a society or association, although offsite, is a direct responsibility on the library-information unit. Membership figures have been shown in both the hardcore and offsite tables in consequence. In this table membership figures are only included in the two asterisked sectors. Comparison of the two sets of figures for "societies" clearly show why this form of result presentation was necessary. The situation of the society or association service alters dramatically for the worse when one includes the membership. A false impression of an easy life is given by only including onsite staff in the core population. The potentially stressed state of the society unit is only equalled by that of the medical service.
Membership figures are again atypical in that one can not distinguish within the whole membership the potential user sector. Any and every member is a potential user. Therefore the membership figures added to both potential user and "total payroll" (or total theoretically relevant population) are of necessity the same.
[2] Library-information worker is here broadly defined to mean of any kind (qualified or unqualified) and at any level or grade.
[3] Services with a pure information function have the lowest staff to user ratios.

Table 12 Hard core ratios—professionally qualified library-information staff

	One qualified[1] library-information worker to...		
	Actual users	Potential users	Total onsite payroll
Whole sample-staff only	194	469	927
– plus members	324	597	1055
Area			
North	188	377	736
Midlands	229	480	1751
South	181	471	819
Type			
Industry, Commerce	197	428	1074
Government	249	633	1096
Society-staff only	55	113	201
– plus members	596	37553	37642
Service title			
Library	243	649	1264
Information	55	141	239
Combined	184	364	756
Different	73	153	360
Medical v rest			
Medical	541	1107	2133
Non-medical	141	370	740

[1] Qualified here means specifically in librarianship and/or information science/studies.

Table 13 Normative hard core population data base for ratio derivation

	Average number per unit of . . .				
	All kinds library-information staff	Qualified library-information staff	Actual users	Potential users	Total onsite payroll
Whole sample	5.2	1.5	291	703	1390
Area					
North	5.3	1.4	263	528	1031
Midlands	3.3	1.1	252	528	1926
South	5.5	1.7	307	800	1392
Type					
Industry, Commerce	3.8	1.1	217	471	1181
Government	7.0	2.0	497	1265	2191
Society-staff	4.7	1.6	88	180	322
Service title					
Library	4.7	1.5	365	973	1896
Information	9.7	2.1	115	297	502
Combined	4.3	1.4	258	509	1058
Different	8.2	1.9	138	291	684
Medical v rest					
Medical	3.1	1.1	595	1218	2346
Non-medical	5.7	1.6	226	592	1184

Table 14 Normative ratios: the wider population – offsite and bona fide users versus all library-information staff

	Av.no. lib-inf. staff per unit	Offsite only				Total population (offsite & onsite)			
		Actual users		Potential		Actual users		Potential	
		Average no. per unit	Ratio 1:	Average no. per unit	Ratio 1:	Average no. per unit	Ratio 1:	Average no. per unit	Ratio 1:
Whole sample	5.2	1185	(228)	24360	(4685)	1476	(284)	25063	(4820)
Industry, Commerce	3.8	397	(104)	4973	(1309)	614	(162)	5444	(1433)
Government	7.0	273	(39)	24161	(3452)	770	(110)	25426	(3632)
Society	4.7								
– members only		865	(184)	59905	(12746)	–	–	–	–
– other offsite only		3554	(756)	4156	(884)	–	–	–	–
– total offsite		4419	(940)	64061	(13630)	4507	(959)	64241	(13668)

Table 15 Normative ratios: the wider population – offsite and bona fide users versus qualified library-information staff

	Av.no. lib-inf. staff per unit	Offsite only				Total population (offsite & onsite)			
		Actual users		Potential		Actual users		Potential	
		Average no.per unit	Ratio 1:	Average no.per unit	Ratio 1:	Average no.per unit	Ratio 1:	Average no.per unit	Ratio 1:
Whole sample	1.5	1185	(790)	24360	(16240)	1476	(984)	25063	(16709)
Industry, Commerce	1.1	397	(358)	4973	(4521)	614	(558)	5444	(4949)
Government	2.0	273	(137)	24161	(12081)	770	(385)	25426	(12713)
Society	1.6								
– members only		865	(541)	59905	(37441)	—	—	—	—
– other offsite only		3554	(2221)	4156	(2598)	—	—	—	—
– total offsite		4419	(2762)	64061	(40038)	4507	(2817)	64241	(40151)

Comments on the normative wider population tables

These tables incorporate the data on which the ratios are based, but confine examination to a single dimension of cross-analysis – by type of parent organisation. There were good reasons for this different mode of presentation. Although these sets of figures are likely to be of great interest to library information managers, they represent a different order of reality from the inhouse user population data (both actual and potential). Information provided – particularly relating to potential outside populations – draws more on intuition, hunch, judgment and guesswork on the part of the respondent than was the case with onsite data. The exception is the membership society or association, where membership figures do reflect reality, though "bona fide" may not.

Nevertheless, offsite material was considered worth presentation, for two reasons. There is a need for information of this kind. In the absence of firm data, which could be impossible (or at least impossibly expensive and time consuming to acquire), any indicators may be useful. The figures emerging in Tables 14–15 also indicate that any organisation would be unwise to plan solely on the basis of the inhouse onsite population. This represents only the tip of the iceberg of the total user population. Even industrial and commercial organisations have substantial offsite user groups (though distance may mercifully diminish the frequency of demand cf. onsite users). So take these figures with a grain of salt, for what they are. At worst they may be regarded as pseudo-quantitation, at best as a useful indicator of rough orders of magnitude.

4.2 "Ideal" ratios

Table 16 Ideal ratios to run present service properly for core population

	Desirable no. lib.-inf. staff (all kinds)	*Average number per unit of...		
		Actual users	Potential users	Total onsite payroll
Whole sample				
– staff only	5.8	291 (50)	703 (121)	1390 (240)
– plus members	5.8	486 (84)	895 (154)	1583 (273)
Area				
North	5.8	263 (45)	528 (91)	1031 (178)
Midlands	3.7	252 (68)	528 (143)	1926 (521)
South	6.2	307 (50)	800 (129)	1392 (225)
Type				
Industry, Commerce	4.2	217 (52)	471 (112)	1181 (281)
Government	7.9	497 (63)	1265 (160)	2191 (277)
Society – staff only	5.4	88 (16)	180 (33)	322 (60)
– plus members	5.4	953 (176)	60085 (11127)	60227 (11153)
Service title				
Library	5.3	365 (70)	973 (192)	1896 (358)
Information	10.3	115 (11)	297 (29)	502 (49)
Combined	4.9	258 (53)	509 (104)	1058 (216)
Different	9.5	138 (15)	291 (31)	684 (72)
Medical v rest				
Medical	3.7	595 (161)	1218 (329)	2346 (634)
Non-medical	6.3	226 (36)	592 (94)	1184 (188)

[1] Ratios are given in brackets after the average number of users per unit. Bracketed figures represent the user side of the ratio and in all cases are set against one library-information worker of any kind.

Table 17 Ideal ratios to expand service to present core population

	Desirable no. lib.-inf. staff (all kinds)	¹Average number per unit of...		
		Actual users	Potential users	Total onsite payroll
Whole sample				
– staff only	6.8	291 (43)	703 (103)	1390 (204)
– plus members	6.8	486 (71)	895 (132)	1583 (233)
Area				
North	6.8	263 (39)	528 (78)	1031 (152)
Midlands	4.7	252 (54)	528 (112)	1926 (410)
South	7.2	307 (43)	800 (111)	1392 (193)
Type				
Industry, Commerce	5.0	217 (43)	471 (94)	1181 (236)
Government	9.0	497 (55)	1265 (141)	2191 (243)
Society – staff only	6.5	88 (14)	180 (28)	322 (50)
– plus members	6.5	953 (148)	60085 (9244)	60227 (9266)
Service title				
Library	6.3	365 (58)	973 (154)	1896 (301)
Information	11.3	115 (10)	297 (26)	502 (44)
Combined	5.8	258 (44)	509 (88)	1058 (182)
Different	11.0	138 (13)	291 (26)	684 (62)
Medical v rest				
Medical	4.5	595 (132)	1218 (271)	2346 (521)
Non-medical	7.4	226 *(31)*¹	592 (80)	1184 (160)

¹ Almost spot on the mythical 1:30 ratio cited for so many years. It is only the medical sector which raises the whole sample average to 1:43. The actual non-medical average is 1:30.54.

Table 18 Ideal ratios to run present service properly for core and wider population combined

	Desirable no. lib.-inf. staff	Average number* per unit of...	
		Actual users	Potential users
Whole sample	5.8	1476 (254)	25063 (4321)
Industry, Commerce	4.2	614 (146)	5444 (1296)
Government	7.9	770 (97)	25426 (3218)
Society	5.4	4507 (835)	64241 (11896)

* Ratios follow in brackets. Each represents the number of users per one library – information worker.

Table 19 Ideal ratios to expand services to present core and wider population combined

	Average number* per unit of . . .		
	Desirable no. lib-inf. staff	Actual users	Potential users
Whole sample	6.8	1476 (217)	25063 (3686)
Industry, Commerce	5.0	614 (123)	5444 (1089)
Government	9.0	770 (86)	25426 (2825)
Society	6.5	4507 (693)	64241 (9883)

* Ratios follow in brackets. Each represents the number of users per one library – information worker.

4.3 Workload ratios

Table 20 Actual traffic or workload ratios: based on enquiries and borrowings on test day

	Average number[1] per unit of . . .		
	Lib.-inf-staff (Total)	Enquiries	Borrowings[2]
Whole sample	5.2	33 (6.3)	26 (5.0)
Area			
North	5.3	25 (4.7)	33 (6.2)
Midlands	3.3	25 (7.6)	23 (7.0)
South	5.5	36 (6.5)	24 (4.4)
Type			
Industry, Commerce	3.8	26 (6.8)	17 (4.5)
Government	7.0	41 (5.9)	39 (5.6)
Society	4.7	31 (6.6)	19 (4.0)
Service title			
Library	4.7	33 (7.0)	30 (6.4)
Information	9.7	32 (3.3)	18 (1.9)
Combined	4.3	32 (7.4)	21 (4.9)
Different	8.2	34 (4.1)	28 (3.4)
Medical v rest			
Medical	3.1	30 (9.7)	28 (9.0)
Non-medical	5.7	33 (5.8)	25 (4.4)

[1] Bracketed figures following averages represent the workload side of the ratio, one library-information worker per so many enquiries or loans per day.
[2] Based on all who answered, including 22 units who in fact have a non-lending policy.

5. The Services

5.1 Descriptive data (sample composition)

The nature of the received sample is shown in the following Tables 21–24. A question that should always be addressed to any received sample is: how typical or representative is it of the parent population from which it was drawn. In this case the parent population was the special sector of the DES Census listing. Structural comparisons of received sample and parent population are provided in Table 24.

Comparison on all factors was not always possible e.g. the DES Census did not distinguish between medical and non-medical services in their analysis.

Separate figures are provided here for the medical field. Presentation of findings in the main body of the report also distinguishes between medical and non-medical services as one of the standard cross-analysis frames.

Reasons for this distinction (the only one made by subject) include widespread belief, backed by observation, that medical services do represent a deprived area of library-information work and provision. Some systematically collected evidence does exist to back up popular belief – e.g. McHugh, P. Continuing education needs of medical library personnel in the UK. London, Ealing College of Higher Education, 1979. Slater, M. Career patterns and the occupational image, London, Aslib, 1979.

Incidentally, in this present survey, medical service does not just mean a hospital library. It includes societies and research establishments in the field, even a few firms producing only medical products and supplies.

One classification scheme or analysis frame applied to participating units and used as a standard cross-analysis frame was size of parent organisation. Size refers to onsite total staff complement, the total payroll figure, used in ratio calculation as the widest in-house user boundary to demarcate the "theoretically possible" population to be served *onsite*. It does not refer to library-information unit staff size and should not be confused with that figure or measure. In some cases the two data sets (organisational and service size) may correlate roughly, but in others they most emphatically do not – e.g. medical, society and association library-information services. To underline the distinction, the category organisational size has been called "Parent organisation" in table headings, rather than simply "size". The latter might have lead to confusion with service size, particularly for readers just dipping casually into this report.

This category, organisational size, is also the one analysis frame that may appear (even to the persevering sequential reader) to have been used irregularly or intermittently throughout the report. It is used as a standard analysis frame for all non-ratio "background" data. It is not however used as an analysis frame for the ratios themselves. The reason for this apparent variation is simple. Organisational size is implicit in the ratios themselves. It would have been a tautologous activity to analyse data based on size by size – rather like solemnly analysing geographical area by area under another name.

Organisational size was used to analyse other background data for two seemingly good reasons. Because it is akin to ratio data, it builds an element or ratio component into these other tables. It was also used in this way because people in our field tend to think in compatible terms. At any gathering of library-information workers one hears discussion of the typical but different situation or problems of the small versus the large organisation.

Defining organisational size categories proved to be a surprisingly difficult task. What is small, for instance and where does large begin in numerical terms? Ad hoc subjective decisions by the author seemed highly undesirable. Yet finally, this was what the author was unwillingly forced to do. In the absence of a single official standard definition of organisational size and in the presence of varying official opinion, I just had to inform myself as fully as I could and then construct my own size categories, as follows:

Mini = up to 50 (employees onsite)*
Small = 51–200
Medium = 201–1,000
Large = over 1,000

Official sources consulted included: the Department of Employment; the Small Firms Division of the Department of Industry; the Training Services Division of the Manpower Services Commission. As indicated, a neat universal official definition of small, medium and large did not emerge from this search.

Actually, there is good reason for the different kinds and bases of classification used by these establishments. To sum it up simply: in some contexts it is sensible to measure in human (or labour-intensivity) terms; in others physical output (production) or finance (turnover) may be more meaningful measures of organisational "size".

Consider industry and commerce. A rich and powerful commercial unit in Central London may be smaller in human or payroll terms than a struggling factory slowly going bankrupt on the outskirts of a provincial town. To compare the two in purely labour-intensive terms is comparing the incomparable.

---

*Working or based at the same site as the participating library-information service.

Hansard (21 June 1979) officially records that there is no single definition of size of organisation and no standard. For some purposes 1–25 or 1–100 may be considered small. It depends on the type of firm. The *Hansard* record adds that sometimes size is measured in terms of turnover, not employees.

Readers who are really interested in pursuing this confused and confusing subject are also referred to the Bolton Report 1971 and its update 1977 (Report of the Committee of enquiry on small firms, presented to Parliament 1971. Command paper 4811). The Walton Committee report of March 1979 is also relevant (or irrelevant, depending on your viewpoint, as it also examines but does not settle the size issue). A short unpublished (but available on request) document from the Manpower Services Commission Training Services Division, grapples manfully with the problem. It is entitled: "The provision of compatible manpower statistics", 1978 (12pp). It states:

"The following employment size bands are recommended as being consistent with the published statistics from the Censuses of Employment and of Production.

Under 11	50–99	500–999
11–24	100–199	1,000+
25–49	200–499	Total

It should be borne in mind that statistics from other sources may well be obtained from establishments or units defined in a particular way, so that comparisons need to be made with due caution".

This classification scheme however provides too many bands for our purposes of cross-analysis. As it stands, it also seems inapplicable to the library-information field context. Small firms in the first two bands described would be most unlikely to have a library-information service at all.

Although percentage differences between our received sample and the parent sample from which it self-selected itself are not gross, they are real and not attributable to chance. Both area and type of organisation figures were tested for significance (χ^2, corrected for continuity in view of disparate size of responder and non-responder groups). As far as area was concerned, differences between received sample and non-responders are highly significant, extremely unlikely to be caused by change. (adjusted $\chi^2 = 16.95$; d.f. = 2, P = <0.001). Heaviest contributions to the value of χ^2 came from the North and South, the Midlands making minimal contribution.

Organisational type differences between responders and non-responders were also highly significant. (Adjusted $\chi^2 = 25.10$; d.f. = 2; P = <0.001). Heavy response to our questionnaire by societies, associations and other similar institutions was the cause. Perhaps such institutions have a fellow feeling for Aslib as another association? Heavy contribution to the value of χ^2 was made by this group, a small contribution by industry-commerce, and a minimal

Table 21 Structure of our received sample

	Total	Industry commerce	Government etc.	Society etc.
Base (100%)	655	277	242	136
Area				
North	144 (22%)	54 (19%)	63 (26%)	27 (20%)
Midlands	88 (13%)	38 (14%)	36 (15%)	14 (10%)
South	423 (65%)	185 (67%)	143 (59%)	95 (70%)
Parent organisation				
Mini	106 (16%)	25 (9%)	16 (7%)	65 (48%)
Small	151 (23%)	74 (27%)	42 (17%)	35 (26%)
Medium	225 (34%)	109 (39%)	97 (40%)	19 (14%)
Large	147 (22%)	66 (24%)	75 (31%)	6 (4%)
Size unknown	26 (4%)	3 (1%)	12 (5%)	11 (8%)
Service title				
Library	327 (50%)	91 (33%)	157 (65%)	79 (58%)
Information	52 (8%)	30 (11%)	11 (5%)	11 (8%)
Combined[1]	238 (36%)	135 (49%)	67 (28%)	36 (26%)
Different[2]	38 (6%)	21 (8%)	7 (3%)	10 (7%)

[1] Service combining "library" and "information" in title,
[2] Some different title, usually an information unit under another name, or a different unit supplying information.

Table 22 Detailed listing of organisational type categories

Base	655(100%)	
Industrial-Commercial		277(42%)
Industry	236(36%)	
Commerce	41(6%)	
Government etc. — central and local		242(37%)
Nationalised industry	27(4%)	
Public corporation	13(2%)	
Government department or agency	188(29%)	
Local government	14(2%)	
Society, association, other		136(21%)
Research or development association	48(7%)	
Learned or professional society	71(11%)	
Other (Charitable, religious, political, etc)	17(3%)	

Table 23 Medical versus non-medical services

	Whole sample	Medical	Non-medical
Base (100%)	655	128	527
Area			
North	22%	29 (23%)	115 (22%)
Midlands	13%	24 (19%)	64 (12%)
South	65%	75 (59%)	348 (66%)
Parent organisation			
Mini	16%	10 (8%)	96 (18%)
Small	23%	17 (13%)	134 (25%)
Medium	34%	46 (36%)	179 (34%)
Large	22%	42 (33%)	105 (20%)
Size unknown*	4%	13 (10%)	13 (2%)
Type			
Industry, Commerce	42%	12 (9%)	265 (50%)
Government, etc.	37%	102 (80%)	140 (27%)
Society, other	21%	14 (11%)	122 (23%)
Service title			
Library	50%	97 (76%)	230 (44%)
Information	8%	5 (4%)	47 (9%)
Combined	36%	25 (20%)	213 (40%)
Different	6%	1 (1%)	37 (7%)

*Probably large.

(Comment on Table 23: based on the evidence of our sample, the typical medical service would appear to be a library. Information provision was low compared with the rest of the sample. Other tables and sections also demonstrate that the typical medical service was an *understaffed* library, vis-a-vis user populations, actually served and potential (*See also* sections 4, 6, 8, 12). This trend is foreshadowed here, in a more loosely defined way, in the size of parent organisation analysis.)

Table 24 Comparison with parent population

	Parent population*	Responders (received sample)	Non-responders
Base (100%)	2,100	655	1,445
Area			
North	567 (27%)	144 (22%)	423 (29%)
Midlands	315 (15%)	88 (13%)	227 (16%)
South	1,218 (58%)	423 (65%)	795 (55%)
Type			
Industry, Commerce	987 (47%)	277 (42%)	710 (49%)
Government	798 (38%)	242 (37%)	556 (39%)
Society, other	315 (15%)	136 (21%)	179 (12%)

*Sample of special services drawn from DES Census listing (addresses to which questionnaire mailed).

one by government services. In other words, here only over-response by societies, etc. seems to have pulled the proportions out of line.

Does this finding, that responders and non-responders to our survey differed significantly on two factors, area and type, invalidate our wider findings (results of the survey)? To answer this question one needs to make a clear distinction, between the concepts of significance and size, between real or significant differences and large ones. Differences can be quite small yet real and not caused by chance – (confirmed minor trend rather than landslide or avalanche). It is in this category of small though real that differences in our sample seem to belong.

Certainly, these differences may mean that our findings for the sample as a whole viewed as a single group, are less reliable than those for each sub-sector within it. Readers should bear this in mind throughout. Differences are not however so large that either the whole received sample or any sub-group within it becomes suspect or unusable.

Another highly possible explanation exists, however, for discrepancy between proportions of sub-groups in the Aslib sample and parent population listing. The reason is timeslip. The two groups could each represent accurately the library-information scene – at two different points in time, or at two different stages of its history. To explain that seemingly curious statement: the DES Census address listing represents the community (at the latest) of 1976. Probably, as it was the recruiting list for the 1976 Census, it actually represents the internal structuring of that community at an even earlier time. Our received sample in this survey came from the community of late 1979. It is known that the number of employed library-information workers, and the number and location of sites employing them, has been changing in recent years. Changes (mainly in the direction of decrease) reflect the influence of external factors, such as general employment levels, economic conditions and the impact of technological innovation.

So it is quite possible that some of our apparent "non-responders" were actually "non-existers" in the world of late 1979. Some evidence for this view did in fact emerge. Letters from management were received stating that "we no longer have a library at our ... branch (or works)". Even more sinister were some returned by GPO packets ("gone away", "not known at this address") indicating the closure of a whole branch or perhaps even organisation.

Societies and associations, although conventionally considered vulnerable as membership organisations in times of economic adversity, may in fact retain their library-information services until the end, until the organisation itself crumbles. Libraries and information units are traditionally services which attract and retain membership. So shaky societies may be less likely to axe them than are industrial-commercial concerns in difficulties. The latter will view their library-information units as more disposable (in the short term) in the cause of immediate survival.

This hypothesis, that perhaps our received sample may not be atypical of the library-information world of 1979–80, is a comforting and not unreasonable one. Unfortunately it is also currently unproveable, awaiting as we do another DES Census.

5.2 Formal service title versus actual function

Early in the questionnaire, as part of "classification data" gathering, we asked respondents two mutually illuminative questions. What was the official or formal title of their service? What was its actual function: what name best described what it actually did? Cross-analysis of these two questions sheds light on management perceptions of the service and the viewpoint of the person actually running it. To what extent did the name given by an employer to a unit reflect or correlate with its actual function within the organisation – as visualised and implemented by the person in charge of that unit? Not perfectly, as Tables 25–26 indicate.

Table 25 Title versus actual function

		Title of Service			
	Whole sample	Library	Information	Combined	Different
Base (100%)	655	327	52	238	38
Function ...					
Library	101 (15%)	**100 (31%)**	—	1 (9%)	—
Information	22 (3%)	4 (1%)	**15 (29%)**	2 (1%)	1 (3%)
Combined Library-Information	467 (71%) (65=10%)	215 (66%) (8=2%)	28 (54%) (9=17%)	**216 (91%)** (19=8%)	8 (21%) **(29=76%)**
(DIFFERENT)					
Information plus different activity	23 (4%)	—	4 (8%)	10 (4%)	9 (24%)
Library plus different activity	7 (1%)	4 (1%)	—	—	3 (8%)
Combined Library-Information plus different activity	35 (5%)	4 (1%)	5 (10%)	9 (4%)	17 (45%)

Table 26 Comparison of function and title percentages for whole sample

	Title	Function
Library	50%	15%
Information	8%	3%
Combined service	36%	71%
Different	6%	10%

Correspondence between title and function was particularly poor in the case of the terms "information" (unit, service etc) and "library". Only in the case of the "combined" library-information service was there good correlation (91% correspondence) of title and function. The "different" group also enjoyed a very fair level of correspondence (76%) of recognition in title and function perception that there was "more to" the unit concerned than library-information provision.

Unfortunately it was not possible to test the results of the analysis displayed in Table 25 for significance. The small number of units claiming a pure information function made this impossible. Expected frequencies in two cells of the table were too low in consequence.

Nevertheless, indicative findings give cause for thought about current and recent christening policies within organisations. Personally, and for quite other reasons, I had in recent years been coming to the reluctant conclusion that the term library should not be lightly or generously bestowed on services – if any other conceivable alternatives existed. Reasons for this belief were based on research in a different area – the occupational image of library and librarian and the comparative status of libraries, information units and other departments within organisations. It is interesting to see what may be additional support for such a view emerging from a quite different data set.

6. Staffing Structures

Material directly and indirectly related to the library-information side of the staff to user trade-off is collected and considered here as a separate issue. It may be of interest and have comparative, indicative or guidance value for people working in the various types of service used as factors in our analyses. A word of warning is perhaps necessary. Tables presenting staff size alone will tell the reader that certain kinds of unit are typically and comparatively larger or smaller. This should not be confused with the issue of understaffing. To know whether a certain kind of unit is prone to understaffing, the number of users must be taken into account as well. Ideally the number, nature and level of services provided to them should also be considered. But this gets complicated. So the reader will need to consult the staff to user ratio tables presented earlier in section 4 Tables 11–20. Information contained in the sections covering non-routine service provision and mechanisation (sections 13, 14) should also be examined.

This section (6) is an internally oriented look at the service itself. It is concerned with staffing structures and typical patterns of staff composition. It leaves the user temporarily out of the picture.

6.1 Staff size and composition

Average size of unit in terms of total staff complement, and composition in terms of qualifications and grades (broadly defined) are examined here. Table 27 draws this material together. This table gives averages expressed in absolute figures, which may be useful for ready reference. Certain trends inherent in the data are not however particularly easy to see in this format. The reader would need to do minor calculations, which can be irritating and time-consuming. So Tables 28 and 29 are also provided. In them, these clarifying sums have already been done, on the pooled staff totals for each type of service (i.e. standard cross-analysis). The total staff pool for each kind of service was taken to represent 100%. Numbers in the various staff categories in each kind of service are expressed as a percentage of the total concerned.

This re-presentation of the data proved a worthwhile exercise. Trends do show up clearly in these Tables 28–29 that are worth comment.

Concerning grading, level of employment (Table 28), fewer professional posts existed in the North of England. The South was curiously low on semi-professional staff, compensatorily high on support. Government services employed comparatively fewer people in professional jobs than societies or profit-making organisations. The combined library-information service was a rather top-heavy unit. It had plenty of Chiefs and Braves, but comparatively fewer lowest level support Indians. The medical service also showed a top-heavy structure, probably because it was usually small in size.

All these differences commented on and others observable in Table 28 are highly unlikely to be caused by chance. Each sector of the table was tested for significance on the raw figures using χ^2 (adjusted where necessary for disproportionately sized groups). All these tests produced a highly significant finding. $P = <0.001$ in all cases.

Forgetting the post occupied and considering the actual qualifications possessed, differences between sub-groups of the sample again emerged (see Table 29). Highest levels of totally unqualified people were found at the two organisational size extremes – in very small and very large parent institutions. This probably reflects inevitable and/or more generous proliferation of support staff in large organisations and possibly the secretary-librarian syndrome in some miniscule organisations.

The Society service would seem to have the highest level of qualified staff and Government units the lowest. A service with an information function – partial or entire – implied by its title, tended to have more qualified staff than a unit whose title implied a pure library function.

The qualification possessed by the information worker was not necessarily however a library-information one (see ensuing discussion of library-information versus "other" qualifications).

Comments so far made on Table 29 are based just on a "no qualification at all" versus "any or some qualification" distinction. For comparison of levels of library-information versus other degrees, diplomas, etc. the reader is referred to the two right-hand columns of Table 29. Trends there indicate that the larger the parent organisation, the more likely it is that formal library-information qualifications will be possessed by staff. The Society service and services whose title implied a library function – partial or entire – were more likely to have heavier representation of library-information qualifications.

Results of Table 29 were also tested for significance. This was only possible on the some qualifications versus no qualifications at all simple distinction basis (because of dual qualification amongst some of the qualified). Not all apparent differences between different types of service were significant. Geographical area differences were below significance level (adjusted $\chi^2 = 4.29$; d.f. $= 2$; $P = 0.20$ approx). The same was true of medical versus non-medical services (adjusted $\chi^2 = 1.55$; d.f. $= 1$; $P = 0.30$ approx). Differences by size and type of parent organisation and by service title were however highly significant.

Table 27 Actual staffing structures[1] in different kinds of organisations and services

	Staff total	Prof. jobs	Semi-prof.	Support jobs	Lib-inf[3] quals.	Other[3] quals.	No quals.
Whole sample	5.2	2.2	1.5	1.5	1.5	1.2	2.8
Area							
North	5.3	2.1	1.9	1.3	1.4	1.3	3.0
Midlands	3.3	1.4	1.1	0.8	1.1	0.9	1.6
South	5.5	2.4	1.4	1.7	1.7	1.2	3.0
Parent organisation							
Mini	4.7	1.9	1.2	1.6	1.0	1.4	2.6
Small	4.0	1.8	1.0	1.2	1.0	1.1	2.1
Medium	4.0	1.8	1.4	0.8	1.4	1.0	2.0
Large	7.6	3.2	1.9	2.5	2.5	1.3	4.3
Size unknown[2]	10.3	3.5	3.8	3.0	2.6	2.1	6.3
Type							
Industry, Commerce	3.8	1.7	1.2	0.9	1.1	1.0	1.9
Government etc.	7.0	2.7	1.8	2.5	2.0	1.3	4.2
Society, other	4.7	2.4	1.3	1.0	1.6	1.3	2.1
Service title							
Library	4.7	1.8	1.5	1.4	1.5	0.8	2.7
Information	9.7	3.9	2.2	3.6	2.1	3.0	5.5
Combined	4.3	2.1	1.3	0.9	1.4	1.0	2.1
Different	8.2	3.3	1.5	3.4	1.9	2.7	4.0
Medical v rest							
Medical	3.1	1.4	1.2	0.5	1.1	0.6	1.6
Non-medical	5.7	2.4	1.6	1.7	1.6	1.3	3.1

[1] All figures given are averages per unit for type of unit concerned. Data was sought late in 1979.
[2] Probably large, which could be the reason why respondents did not know total payroll size. Size refers to total number of employees at same site as responding library-information unit.
[3] Overlap occurs between these two-columns. A staff member may possess a library-information qualification *and* some other qualification. So columns 1-3 here add up to more than total.

Table 28 Grade percentages in various service categories*

	Total staff pool (100%)	Professional jobs %	Semi-professional %	Support jobs %
Whole sample	3390.5	43	28	29
Area				
North	760.5	39	36	25
Midlands	287	44	33	23
South	2343	44	25	31
Parent organisation				
Mini	502.5	41	26	33
Small	603.5	46	24	30
Medium	900	45	34	31
Large	1117.5	42	25	33
Size unknown	267	34	37	29
Type				
Industry, Commerce	1057.5	45	33	22
Government	1691	38	26	36
Society, other	642	51	27	22
Service title				
Library	1540	40	31	29
Information	507.5	40	23	37
Combined	1030.5	50	30	20
Different	312.5	40	18	42
Medical v rest				
Medical	395.5	46	38	16
Non-medical	2994	42	27	31

* Frozen posts are not included. This represents a head count of staff in post, although part-timers are expressed in full-time equivalent terms.

Table 29 Qualifications – percentages

	None %	Some %	Type of qualification*... Library information %	Other %
Whole sample	54	46	30	23
Area				
North	56	44	26	24
Midlands	49	51	34	27
South	54	46	30	22
Parent organisation				
Mini	55	45	22	29
Small	52	48	25	27
Medium	50	50	35	25
Large	57	43	33	17
Size unknown	61	39	25	21
Type				
Industry, Commerce	50	50	29	27
Government	60	40	28	18
Society, other	46	54	35	27
Service title				
Library	58	42	32	18
Information	56	44	21	31
Combined	49	51	33	23
Different	49	51	23	32
Medical v rest				
Medical	51	49	36	20
Non-medical	55	45	29	23

* Percentages in these two columns add up to more than the total of qualified people, as dual qualification possession occurred.

The composition of the total "special" staff pool or workforce (as represented by our sample) was considered in Tables 28–29. Adopting a different view point Tables 30–31 examine the typical patterns or combinations of staff qualification encountered within individual units or services. The four mutually exclusive pattern structures encountered can be summed up as: totally unqualified staff (in any formal sense); possibly relevant "subject qualifications" only – no library-information qualifications possessed; library-information qualifications only – no additional relevant or irrelevant other degrees or diplomas; mixture of library-information and other qualifications possessed by staff of the unit concerned.

The proportions of these four patterns or structures within our sample of units as a whole is shown first in a simple summary Table 30. Details of the distribution of the four structures amongst the sub-groups of the sample are provided in Table 31. As this is a large table, drawing together a lot of numerical material, display is restricted to percentages only in the interests of comprehensibility.

Raw data (absolute figures) were tested for significance. Although the table presents full results for all the standard cross-sorts or sub-groups of the sample, readers should be warned that not all the apparent differences are statistically significant. Geographical area and the medical versus non-medical comparison are cases in point. Apparently these were not factors influencing or relating to patterns or combinations of qualification within services at the time of our study. Area χ^2 (adjusted) = 2.04; d.f. = 6; P = 0.70 approximately, which is well below significance level. Medical versus non-medical services χ^2 (adjusted) = 5.08; d.f. = 3; P = 0.20 approximately, again below significance level.

Factors which did relate causally to qualification patterns within units were size of parent organisation, type of organisation and service title. Correlation was particularly strong in the case of the last two factors. It will be noted that these three factors are themselves related, on a commonsense basis, as being organisational in nature. Even the service title is usually something decided and bestowed by the employer.

Concerning the size of the parent organisation; $\chi^2 = 18.29$; d.f. = 9; P = 0.03 approximately. Differences are significant, but not highly so. The small "size unknown" group had to be excluded from this test. Type of organisation $\chi^2 = 18.02$; d.f. = 6; P = <0.001. Differences are highly significant. Service title χ^2 (adjusted) = 30.65; d.f. = 9; P = <0.001. Differences again are highly significant. In this case (service title) the greatest contributions to the value of χ^2 came from the separate Libraries and Information Units. Minimal contribution was made by the combined library-information units.

Table 30. General staff composition descriptors: summary

655 (100%)	Base (units or services not people)
120 (18%)	Nobody with any qualifications (of any kind) on the staff of the unit
104 (16%)	Only qualifications possessed are not library-information ones.
204 (31%)	Only library-information qualifications represented.
227 (35%)	A mix of library-information and other qualifications are represented.

Note: the last three categories do not imply that everybody on the staff is so qualified, just that such qualification is represented by at least one member of staff in the unit concerned.

Table 31   General staff composition descriptors: sub-group analysis

	Base* (100%)	Type of qualification			
		None %	Only other %	Only lib-inf. %	Mix %
Whole sample	655	18	16	31	35
Area					
North	144	20	16	31	33
Midlands	88	20	19	31	30
South	423	17	15	31	36
Parent organisation					
Mini	106	18	21	35	26
Small	151	19	21	25	34
Medium	225	20	11	31	38
Large	147	13	13	37	37
Size unknown	26	31	23	23	23
Type					
Industry, Commerce	277	22	20	29	29
Government etc.	242	16	14	35	35
Society, other	136	15	11	29	45
Service title					
Library	327	23	12	34	31
Information	52	6	21	13	60
Combined	238	16	18	33	33
Different	38	13	29	21	37
Medical v rest					
Medical	128	16	15	40	29
Non-medical	527	19	16	29	36

* Percentages run horizontally in this table.

Findings shown in Tables 30–31 strongly indicate the possibility of considerable mismatch between posts and formal qualifications. It is obvious that some services (18%) are managed by people with no formal qualifications of any kind. The figures also indicate that some formally qualified people may be occupying relatively junior posts, perhaps more suited to unqualified people. This issue is explored in more specific detail in the next section (6.2).

So far, comments on the Table sequences 27–29, 30–31 have been fairly detailed and specific. Wider readings and implications are possible and possibly more meaningful. In the context of a profession somewhat troubled about the future, its future, and by questions arising regarding manpower planning, employment prospects, educational policies etc., one might more usefully ask: what do these tables mean?

Prophets of professional doom have interpreted the wider scene in terms of shrinking or vanishing library-information services and few jobs for the emergent graduates of library-information schools. Yet the trends in Tables 28–29 and 30–31 do indicate that some potential exists for taking up external slack *within the current employment framework*. Eighteen percent of the services in our sample were staffed completely by unqualified people. A further 16% had nobody on the staff possessing library-information qualifications (although some staff members had degrees or diplomas in other disciplines). The allied finding that apparently only 30% of the whole staff pool (emerging from the units in our sample) possessed library-information qualifications also indicates that by restructuring within the field more jobs could be liberated for the library school output (past and present) than one might imagine. Of course this might also be beneficial to users and organisations! Later material (see section 6.2, Table 34) confirms the mismatch trend. In some units qualified people or graduates were occupying semi-professional or clerical support posts. In other units unqualified people held down the top or other senior jobs. Now in the latter case they may do so very well. Real-life "qualification" for a "job" (broadly or narrowly defined) is as much a matter of personality, aptitude, motivation and experience as it is of pieces of paper. So my analysis of this situation does not urge adoption of the Attila the Hun management style – i.e. people-directed brutal internal restructuring by weeding of the work-force to achieve what appears to be a worthwhile end.

Rather it advocates the use of natural wastage. Library-information work appears to be a reasonably mobile profession, even in economically adverse times. So this is not a frivolous or unworkable suggestion. In practical terms, employers should pause for thought every time a senior, professional, or even semi-professional post is vacated by an unqualified person. Might the employer not do even better in future by offering this job to someone with library-information qualifications?

This analysis or strategy may seem somewhat naive, on at least two counts. It begs the question of comparative costs of qualified and unqualified staff. In answer, one can only say that employers might do well to think in terms of cost benefit and the quality of goods purchased, not just in terms of price-tags. Library-information workers are not, in any case, exactly over-priced commodities in the labour market in comparison with most other professions and many trades.

The allied explosive issue of the impact of new technology has also been ignored. Technological innovation may reduce the over-all need for professional expertise (as currently defined in our field) per se. At the same time, naive or not, the natural wastage-replacement strategy does seem to offer some kind of positive, if simplistic, partial solution or alleviation of some present employment problems of the profession.

6.2 Mismatch between posts and qualifications

Apparently illogical distribution of qualified person-power within the workforce was indicated by some findings presented in the previous section. Further analysis of the work structure within services revealed that this was in fact the case. In going on for a quarter of the services in our sample, everybody seemed to be in the wrong job – at least as far as their formal qualifications for that job were concerned! Findings are presented in a sequence of three Tables: 32–34. A brief summary of extent of mismatch; an analysis of extent of mismatch in the various sub-groups of the sample; an examination of the nature of mismatch, or the kind of mismatch typically encountered.

In fairness to the reader a couple of simple rules adopted when categorising mismatch should be explained. A logical hard line was taken that a library-information qualification was necessary for a professional library-information job. A library-information qualification or other degree was not however considered necessary for a semi-professional or support job.

Table 32   Extent of mismatch: summary

655 (100%)	Base
151 (23%)	Total mismatch of grades, posts and qualifications – i.e. all cases
269 (41%)	Some degree of mismatch – not all cases
235 (36%)	No obvious mismatch – i.e. no cases

Considerable differences between sub-groups of the sample can be observed in Table 33, as far as mismatch of posts and formal qualifications is concerned. Most of these differences are "real" – i.e. extremely unlikely to be caused by chance.

Geographical siting of the service is the only possible exception. Yet even here it is debatable whether some weak correlation between extent of mismatch and area may not exist. Results of χ^2 test were hovering on the verge of significance. Adjusted $\chi^2 = 8\cdot 34$; d.f. $= 4$; $P = > 0\cdot 05$, but $< 0\cdot 10$.

Size of parent organisation and mismatch of posts are certainly related factors. Differences are highly significant. $\chi^2 = 17\cdot 80$; d.f. $= 6$; $P = < 0\cdot 01$. The small group "size unknown" was excluded from the calculation. It should be noted that medium-sized organisations made minimal contribution to the value of χ^2, actual and expected frequencies being very close (not only to one another, but also to the proportions in the sample viewed as a whole).

Table 33 Extent of mismatch: sub-group analysis

	Base* (100%)	Total mismatch	Some	None
Whole sample	655	151(23%)	269(41%)	235(36%)
Area				
North	144	39(27%)	48(33%)	57(40%)
Midlands	88	27(31%)	33(37%)	28(32%)
South	423	85(20%)	188(44%)	150(36%)
Parent organisation				
Mini	106	32(30%)	31(29%)	43(41%)
Small	151	37(25%)	71(47%)	43(28%)
Medium	225	52(23%)	91(40%)	82(36%)
Large	147	20(14%)	67(45%)	60(41%)
Size unknown	26	10(38%)	9(35%)	7(27%)
Type				
Industry, Commerce	277	76(27%)	126(46%)	75(27%)
Government, etc	242	50(21%)	85(35%)	107(44%)
Society, other	136	25(18%)	58(43%)	53(39%)
Service title				
Library	327	85(26%)	107(33%)	135(41%)
Information	52	6(12%)	34(65%)	12(23%)
Combined	238	46(19%)	112(47%)	80(34%)
Different	38	14(37%)	16(42%)	8(21%)
Medical v rest				
Medical	128	29(23%)	38(30%)	61(47%)
Non-medical	527	122(23%)	231(44%)	174(33%)

* Percentages in this table run horizontally

Type of organisation also related causally to mismatch. Differences were highly significant. $\chi^2 = 18 \cdot 71$; d.f. = 4; P = <0·001. Societies, associations etc. made a noticeably smaller contribution to the value of χ^2 than industry-commerce or government.

Title of service and mismatched posts and qualifications within that service were also related factors. Adjusted $\chi^2 = 28 \cdot 41$; d.f. = 6; P = 0·002 approximately. Differences are highly significant.

Medical services differed significantly from other kinds of service. Although identical levels of total mismatch existed in medical and non-medical services,

Table 34 Nature of mismatch

655 (100%)	Base*
	Professional level jobs – underqualification
76 (12%)	any cases this level with no qualifications of any kind.
174 (27%)	cases where no library-information qualifications, but "other" qualifications possessed.
	Semi-professional level jobs – overqualification and other anomalies
8 (1%)	most highly qualified people on staff are here, while less well qualified people hold the professional jobs.
108 (16%)	downgrading of top post to this level by employer, officially no professional posts exist, semi-professional boss syndrome: all cases, qualified and unqualified.
42 (6%)	as above, but semi-professional boss has a qualification, either library-information and/or other degree, diploma etc.
81 (12%)	other cases of professionally qualified or graduate staff in semi-professional jobs.
	Support staff level – overqualification, other anomalies
32 (5%)	overqualified in any way, possessing library-information or any other qualifications.
14 (2%)	downgrading of top job to this level by employer. Only support staff employed. The clerk-boss syndrome.
4 (1%)	*Any other miscellaneous anomalies not covered above*

* Unlike the "extent" Tables 32–33, Table 34 does not add up to 100%, although it is based on the sample as a whole. This "nature" table reviews the data in the first two "extent" categories (complete and partial mismatch) in more detail. The "none" category is fairly obviously self-excluded. Multiple answers or categorisations were also possible in the "nature" table. More than one type of mismatch can occur in a single service. So (although percentaged on the whole sample base of 655 units), it adds up to neither the 100% total, nor the 64% sub-total of units with partial or total mismatch. Sub-group analysis of Table 34 findings is not presented, as it makes for a very unwieldy format to consult. Readers particularly and seriously interested in these figures and this level of detail are welcome to visit Aslib Research Department and consult the computer printout. If distance is a real hindrance to such a visit they may prefer to write requesting a photocopy of the relevant printout.

there were large differences in the proportions of partial mismatch and apparently perfect match. Adjusted $\chi^2 = 10.43$; d.f. = 2; P = <0.01. Differences are highly significant. No contribution to χ^2 came from the "total mismatch" category.

Curiously enough, the medical service was more likely to have a technically perfect structure (no obvious mismatch of posts and qualifications) than the non-medical service. In operational terms this however hardly compensates for the small staff size of the typical medical service and the large number of users per staff-member.

6.3 Part-time or full-time?

Part-time work is an issue encountered, but so far side-stepped by this report. In the ratio calculations, for example, part-time staff were expressed in manpower terms of full-time equivalency. In other words, three half-timers = 1½ manpower (or womanpower as the case may well be).

In this section the part-time question is examined in isolation in its own right, to see to what extent the various types of organisation and service make any use of part-time workers. Data is presented from a service structure point of view. It distinguishes between units: only employing part-timers; using both part-time and full-time staff; only employing full-time staff.

Table 35   Part-time versus full-time staff

	Base (100%)	Only part-timers %	PT/FT mix %	Only full-timers %
Whole sample	655	65(10%)	123(19%)	467(71%)
Area				
North	144	13	17	70
Midlands	88	13	19	68
South	423	8	19	72
Parent organisation				
Mini	106	19	20	61
Small	151	8	17	75
Medium	225	9	20	71
Large	147	5	18	76
Size unknown	26	15	15	70
Type				
Industry, Commerce	277	6	14	80
Government etc.	242	12	21	67
Society, other	136	14	26	60
Service title				
Library	327	15	19	65
Information	52	2	15	83
Combined	238	4	19	77
Different	38	13	18	68
Medical v rest				
Medical	128	22	25	53
Non-medical	527	7	17	76

As the two groups using part-timers (entirely or partially) were both comparatively small, they were clumped together when testing for significance. So χ^2 tests were based on the simple distinction of using or not using part-timers at all. The first two columns of Table 35 were added together and set against the final column.

On this basis not all the differences within sub-groups proved significant. There would seem to be no association between geographical area and the use of part-time staff. Adjusted $\chi^2=0.5$; d.f.$=2$; P$=0.80$ approximately, which is well below significance level. A weak correlation may (or may not) exist between size of parent organisation and tendency to employ part-timers. Adjusted $\chi^2=6.97$; d.f.$=3$; P$=<0.10$ but >0.05, which is verging on significance level. The small group "size unknown" was excluded from the calculation.

However, when we came to consider type of parent organisation, service title and the medical non-medical service distinction, significant differences did emerge. These were the factors affecting or relating to the employment of part-timers. The industrial-commercial unit seemed particularly unlikely to offer employment to the part-timer. Only 20% of profit making organisations in our sample did so. Societies, associations, etc. were most likely to avail themselves of part-time help. Occasionally this was even voluntary or "honorary". Adjusted $\chi^2=19.34$; d.f.$=2$; P$=<0.001$. Differences are highly significant.

Service title affected the part-time issue in the following way: a service with an implied information function (the information unit or combined service) was markedly less likely to use part-timers than the "pure" library. The small group of "different services" combining library and/or information work with some other official duties was an apparent anomaly. It is highly likely however that the seemingly and relatively high use of part-timers in these "different" services reflects a different kind or definition of part-time work. Not so much people who only work part-time, as people who work full-time, but splitting this time between two functions or even two linked departments. Adjusted χ^2 for the service title analysis$=11.90$; d.f.$=3$; P$=<0.01$. Differences are highly significant. Minimal contribution to the value of χ^2 came from the "different" category in any case. The real differences lie between library, information and combined service.

The medical service would seem to be the real "home from home" of the part-time library-information worker. Forty-seven percent of medical services in our sample made some use of part-time help. Knowledge of the doubling up of jobs syndrome in hospitals (Consultant's Secretary who also "looks after our small library") indicates that once again part-time workers per se may not always be the real issue. However, we also know that in other cases a real part-time worker (who goes home at lunch-time, or only comes in three times a week) is all that is around to help the user. The rest of the week the user presumably helps him or herself. Possibly with disastrous consequences to operational efficiency of the unit and size and location of stock. Or the user may be denied access to the temporarily unstaffed service. Some cases like this were documented in medical and society or association libraries. "When I am not here, the library is (or the book cases are) locked." This phenomenon is equally undesirable from a different point of view. Medical service analysis: adjusted $\chi^2 = 24 \cdot 58$; d.f. $= 1$; $P = = <0 \cdot 001$. Differences are highly significant.

7. A Shrinking Profession?

A direct connection between the material contained in this section and staff to user ratios may not be immediately apparent. Readers might wonder about the sudden intrusion of apparent irrelevancies. The related topics of post freezing and growth or attrition status of the service are however very relevant to the whole wider issue of current and future manpower forecasting and deployment. This report is concerned with and hopefully makes a contribution to this broader subject field.

Within the narrower context of the report's official title, one could also add the frozen posts recorded to the staffing side of the ratios. This might give some idea of what (in better economic circumstances than the present) the employer considered a fair ratio.

The concept of the shrinking profession is also an emotive and much debated topic, generating a considerable amount of panic and/or depression amongst library-information workers. Two major reasons for the "doomwatch" trend are detectable. One is economic and is perceived by the majority as not merely a cause, but as the cause. In times of economic hardship, organisations prune back peripheral functions, departments and people. The library-information unit does not generate any visible product or profit. It is not particularly amenable to cost benefit analysis. So it is rightly perceived as being "at risk". More discerning analysts have detected another influence at work. This is the impact of new technology, the micro revolution, unlike in momentum or potential anything we have previously seen by way of agent for industrial and social change. At the moment the two influences re-inforce one another. But the new technology will be the enduring influence. This is what the doom-watchers really ought to be watching, not the fluctuating state of the economy. Admittedly, it is (and will continue to be) difficult in practice to separate the two.

So any data that illuminates or acts as a monitor on the extent to which posts really are being frozen, or services cut back in any other way, is felt to be worth recording. These topics do seem worth considering, if only briefly.

7.1 Frozen posts

The incidence of frozen posts in the services taking part in our study and the number of posts involved are analysed in Table 36. Sixteen percent of the services in our sample had frozen posts at the time of the study (late 1979). Considering the number of posts likely to be frozen within a unit, the range was from 0·5 (one part-time post) to 13 (in one atypical and large unit).

This range gives a false impression. Actually only 10 out of the 655 units (1·5%) were carrying more than two frozen posts per unit.

Table 36 Frozen posts

	Base* (100%)	None frozen	Some frozen	Average number frozen per unit	
				All units	In units with FPs
Whole sample	655	551(84%)	104(16%)	0.25	1.54
Area		%	%		
North	144	87.5	12.5	0.14	1.14
Midlands	88	91	9	0.09	1.06
South	423	82	18	0.31	1.69
Parent organisation					
Mini	106	92	8	0.08	0.94
Small	151	83	17	0.23	1.35
Medium	225	85	15	0.21	1.40
Large	147	78	22	0.39	1.80
Size unknown	26	88	12	0.46	4.0
Type					
Industry, Commerce	277	89	11	0.13	1.18
Government	242	77	23	0.42	1.83
Society, Other	136	86	14	0.18	1.29
Service title					
Library	327	90	10	0.17	1.63
Information	52	77	23	0.28	1.21
Combined	238	80	20	0.30	1.51
Different	38	74	26	0.47	1.80
Medical v rest					
Medical	128	88	12	0.12	0.97
Non-medical	527	83	17	0.28	1.65

* Percentages run horizontally in this table

Certain factors seemed to be associated with post freezing. Type of organisation and service title would seem to be the influential factors. Government services were much more prone to post freezing than industrial-commerical or "society" services. Adjusted $\chi^2 = 13 \cdot 11$; d.f. = 2; P = 0·002 approximately.

Differences are highly significant. Libraries were less prone to post freezing than services with an implied information function (partial or complete). Adjusted $\chi^2 = 13 \cdot 79$; d.f. = 3; P = < 0·01. Differences are again highly significant. Area and size of parent organisation could possibly have a weak relationship as factors, to post-freezing. In both cases probability was marginally below significance level. Whether the service was in the medical field or not bore no relationship to post freezing. Any apparent difference in this sector of Table 36 can be attributed to chance. Adjusted $\chi^2 = 1 \cdot 06$; d.f. = 1; P = 0·40 approximately, below significance level.

7.2 Growth or attrition?

Respondents were asked whether "during the year prior to receipt of this questionnaire" their "total staff complement" had grown in number, remained the same or shrunk. The large majority of services (76%) had remained the same size. The small growing and shrinking groups were roughly the same size, but it is perhaps comforting that growing services marginally outnumbered shrinking ones (by 2% or 17 units).

The sub-groups of the sample exhibited no significant differences, except in the case of medical versus non-medical services. Apparently this was the only factor associated with growth status of service. Curiously enough medical services would seem to be growing in terms of staff size significantly more than the rest of the special services. A welcome and necessary change in the right direction for a group characterised by small unit size and large user populations.

As there were no significant variations amongst the other sub-groups of the sample the usual full cross analysis is not presented. Table 37 gives results only for the sample as a whole, plus the medical, non-medical cross sort. In this case adjusted $\chi^2 = 8 \cdot 35$: d.f. = 2; P = <0·02. Differences are highly significant.

The group who reported that the service had shrunk in the past year (11%) was smaller than the group reporting frozen posts within the service (16%). This indicates that some frozen posts were of long duration.

Table 37 Growth status of service

	Whole sample	Medical services	Non-medical
Base (100%)	655	128	527
Growing	87 (13%)	23 (18%)	64 (12%)
Static	498 (76%)	100 (78%)	398 (76%)
Shrinking	70 (11%)	5 (4%)	65 (12%)

8. Adequacy of Current Staffing

Adequacy of present staff size and composition were explored in a series of questions. These covered quantitative and qualitative aspects of adequacy, including reasons for qualitative inadequacy or "poor performance".

8.1 Quantitative adequacy

Thinking purely (or as purely as possible) in numerical terms, about staff size in relation to workload, a large group of unit heads (44%) felt that they were understaffed. Findings are additionally depressing in that only 21% seemed to be in a situation that was above survival or coping level. They were the only managers who felt that present staffing levels were sufficient to permit any expansion of services in desirable directions. For the rest (79%), this was out of the question with the present number of staff.

Results for the sample as a whole are provided in Table 38. Detailed findings for sub-groups of the sample are not shown, as there were no significant differences between them.

Table 38 Adequacy of staff size

652 (100%)*	Base
135 (21%)	Adequately staffed to permit some expansion of services provided or to cope with increased demand if necessary.
228 (35%)	Adequately staffed to maintain present level of service and meet current demand but any expansion etc. would be out of the question.
207 (32%)	Slightly understaffed re maintenance of present service provision and meeting current demand.
82 (12%)	Really understaffed re maintenance of present services and meeting demand.

* Three respondents did not answer this question. An "other" answer option was provided, but was not used by respondents. Those who answered were able to do so via the scale supplied.

The original question producing these findings was a "closed" one. Respondents were presented with four verbal descriptors amounting to an adequacy scale. They were asked to select the one which best described their own present situation. The categories or descriptors of Table 38 are those used in the question.

Exploration of staffing level adequacy was not confined solely to current levels. The respondent was also asked to extrapolate, to say what s/he thought a "comfortable but realistic number of staff for your library/information service" would be. Two figures were in fact requested: the number needed to maintain the present service level without stress; the number needed to allow for expansion. Results of this double-barrelled question are shown in Table 39.

Table 39 Actual versus desirable staffing levels

	Actual[1] staff	Total number needed to	
		Maintain present service	Expand, improve
Whole sample	5.2	5.8 (+0.6)[2]	6.8 (+1.6)[2]
Area			
North	5.3	5.8 (0.5)	6.8 (1.5)
Midlands	3.3	3.7 (0.4)	4.7 (1.4)
South	5.5	6.2 (0.7)	7.2 (1.7)
Parent organisation			
Mini	4.7	5.3 (0.6)	6.2 (1.5)
Small	4.0	4.4 (0.4)	5.3 (1.3)
Medium	4.0	4.5 (0.5)	5.4 (1.4)
Large	7.6	8.6 (1.0)	9.8 (2.2)
Size unknown	10.3	11.6 (1.3)	13.1 (2.8)
Type			
Industry, Commerce	3.8	4.2 (0.4)	5.0 (1.2)
Government etc	7.0	7.9 (0.9)	9.0 (2.0)
Society, other	4.7	5.4 (0.7)	6.5 (1.8)
Service title			
Library	4.7	5.3 (0.6)	6.3 (1.6)
Information	9.7	10.3 (0.6)	11.3 (1.6)
Combined	4.3	4.9 (0.6)	5.8 (1.5)
Different	8.2	9.5 (1.3)	11.0 (2.8)
Medical v rest			
Medical	3.1	3.7 (0.6)	4.5 (1.4)
Non-medical	5.7	6.3 (0.6)	7.4 (1.7)

[1] Average number of staff (of all kinds) now working in library-information unit.
[2] Bracketed numbers represent the additional staff required. They were inserted to save readers the chore of doing irritating little sums when consulting the table.

Strictly speaking, this was not a quantitative or factual question. Neither, however, was it a purely subjective or qualitative one. It makes demands on the respondent for joint use of subjective judgment and critical, objective observation or review of past experience as unit head. It is a quantitative–qualitative question.

As answers were expressed in numerical form and as their content was closely allied to, or a projection of factual staff size, results seemed marginally to belong here in the "quantitative" section.

It should also be stressed that this question was tackled by respondents in a realistic and sensible way. It was not taken as an opportunity for wish fulfillment or hypothetical empire-building. The numbers themselves indicate this. They reflect a responsible attitude and response to what must have been a difficult question. Additional evidence, which does not show up in a table of this kind, was afforded by the people who actually cited a slightly *lower* number of staff as capable of maintaining current service levels comfortably. Sometimes this was qualified by "fewer but different". Different here meant a different mix of staff, in terms of experience, qualifications, maturity or personality.

The general trend of Table 39 is clear and shows considerable consistency. To maintain present level of service efficiently and without stress, the average unit needs a part-timer in addition to its existing complement. To expand, improve the service, or add new functions the average unit needs another full-timer (*as well as* the part-timer). To sum up: to maintain present service level – half a person more is needed; to expand and improve – one and a half more people are needed.

Obviously this can (and does) vary somewhat with the type of service. Larger services felt that they needed rather more than the average – e.g. government services and information units. Smaller services felt that they could manage with slightly less than the average – e.g. small organisations and those based in the Midlands. This reflects a rough relation of perceived need to size of current staff and operations.

8.2 Qualitative adequacy

Forgetting numbers and concentrating instead on the kind of people staffing the library-information service, was the unit head really satisfied? Were staff-members the right people for the organisation, the service and their particular job?

Respondents were asked to consider this qualitative aspect of staffing adequacy and to indicate their own situation, using a list of provided statements.

Results, including three final additional categories suggested by respondents themselves, are shown in Table 40. Whole sample findings only are given, as there were no significant differences between the sub-groups of the sample.

Table 40   Qualitative adequacy (performance)

655 (100%)		Base
		Scale supplied on questionnaire
161 (25%)		⎧ All are above average, no complaints at all.
239 (36%)	A*	⎨ All are at least adequate, some of even better standard.
88 (13%)		⎩ All are adequate or satisfactory, but none outstanding.
34 (5%)		⎧ Most are adequate, but some fall below this standard.
15 (2%)		⎪ Most are inadequate or unsuitable in some way, not quite what you would wish.
	B*	⎨ *Additional categories supplied by respondent*
25 (4%)		⎪ Divide sharply into below or above average.
25 (4%)		⎩ Work situation unsatisfactory rather than people involved: external factors causing poor performance.
68 (10%)	C*	Unable or unwilling to rate self (very small units).

* A = satisfactory situations of varying degrees (75%);
 B = unsatisfactory situations of various kinds (15%);
 C = undeclared or unknown situations (10%).

Qualitative assessments of staff adequacy produced a prettier picture of life in the average library-information unit than the quantitative assessments had done. Only 15% of services in our sample seemed to be in a really unsatisfactory situation – i.e. possessing (or carrying) some inadequate or unsuitable staff-members. The majority (61%) seemed to be in a good position, with no inadequate staff and at least some (and sometimes all) staff rated as "above average" quality.

In carrying out tests for significance on the sub-groups of the sample, category C was excluded from the calculation and category B was viewed and used as a single clumped group. Unfortunately this method did not differentiate between degree or kind of inadequacy. It was however necessary, as the finely differentiated "inadequate" combinations within B were too small to use individually. Results of χ^2 tests on this basis (B clumped, C excluded) did not reveal any significant differences between sub-groups.

Reasons for qualitative inadequacy were also explored. Respondents were asked about factors contributing to sub-standard or undesirable work performance. A list of possible causes was provided, but to many respondents this merely acted as a stimulus or starter. Drawing on their own experience they added a few other interesting and valid influences. The resulting mixture is shown in Table 41. Respondent supplied categories are marked.

Table 41 Factors contributing to poor performance

Rank	441 (100%)	Base*
1†	206 (47%)	Context induced low morale; employer's fault: pay, conditions of (over) work, lack of career or promotion prospects, low status.
2	195 (44%)	Motivation low or absent, lack of interest.
3	164 (37%)	Personality just wrong for the job.
4	116 (26%)	Previous work experience or on the job training insufficient or lacking.
5	101 (23%)	Formal qualifications inadequate, irrelevant or poor preparation for the work itself.
6	56 (13%)	Overqualified or underemployed in the particular post.
7†	34 (8%)	Turnover rate in service and its consequences – lack of continuity, over-work, fluctuation in staff quality result.
8†	24 (5%)	Basic intelligence just not up to the job, or specific basic aptitudes lacking (e.g. "can't write, can't spell"; "can't reason, can't plan ahead"). Described by exasperated respondents as "thick and stupid" or "illiterate".
9†	17 (4%)	Age and/or disability: chronic ill-health or fragility can lead to poor performance and attendance (absence rates cited).
9†	17 (4%)	Private commitments, domestic and other outside responsibilities: not available for full-time work (when needed).

* Based on those actually answering, not whole sample percentages.
† Respondent supplied categories not included in the original listing of question 9(b).

In fact the original question was completed exactly as requested by few respondents and added to and amended by many. So a different form of analysis had to be used from that initially intended. The new analysis frame did however still produce a ranked order of priority. It also embraced answers from the "any other factors" extensions of the question.

Before describing the broad positive results of this question, it should be pointed out that in this case a negative result or failure to answer was meaningful. The question was specifically aimed at people with "any current or recent experience of inadequacy or unsuitability". In other words the bitter fruits of experience were sought, not rumour or hearsay from the inexperienced. Thirty-three percent of the sample did not answer the question. Percentages are based on those who did answer, but readers should bear in mind that these are not whole sample percentages.

Let us, however, return to results from the 67% who had experience of staff inadequacy and responded to the question. The employer emerged as the largest single basic cause of poor performance in the employee. The library-information worker was absolved by many from ultimate responsibility for his or her performance at work. This category "context induced low morale and performance, employer's fault" was a respondent supplied concept, which makes its first rank status even more impressive. If it had been listed as a formal given option, it might have scored even more points. A finding of this kind was also pre-shadowed and is reinforced by another respondent supplied answer category that emerged in Table 40. "The whole work situation is unsatisfactory rather than the people involved."

Taking the first, second and third rank factors together builds up a formidable weight of opinion about what really matters. The work environment and personal reaction or ability to adapt to it are what counts in determining staff adequacy. Motivation, morale, personality and innate aptitude were believed to be what really counted in making a good library-information worker. Good potential could however be sabotaged by the environment of the work place itself. Good potential and performance were not viewed basically as matters of formal qualification, training or experience, although these also counted as less important factors influencing performance. Nor were external factors disconnected with the work environment thought to be very influential (e.g. domestic problems or commitments). Such factors were low-ranking in perceived impact on performance.

Did the type of organisation or service have any effect on the perceived relative importance of factors believed to influence or cause staff inadequacy? The broad answer is: not to a great extent and not in all kinds of unit. (There were however some interesting minor differences which will be described shortly).

Size of parent organization, type of organisation and the medical, non-medical distinction revealed no real differences in pattern from that shown by the sample as a whole.

Area or siting of service and its name or official title did show variation. In the Midlands lack of interest on the worker's part was allotted first rank, wrong personality second and employer induced low morale third. Libraries and combined library-information services were more prone to think that poor performance was the employer's fault than were services with a heavier designated information responsibility (i.e. information services and "different" units with an information supply function). Libraries ranked context caused low morale first. Combined services gave a shared first ranking to employer and employee lack of interest in the service and the occupation. Information services blamed the employee, lack of basic interest being ranked first. The "different" services thought that wrong personality for the job was the prime cause.

In all types of service and organisation however the three paramount factors put forward were the same. It was the priorities attached to them that sometimes differed. It should also be pointed out that sometimes the numerical gap or margin between rankings was small and technical rather than large and meaningful.

So to sum up, unit heads saw the major causes of staff inefficiency or inadequacy as: employer attitude reflected in work environment; lack of interest and motivation on the workers' part (possibly and/or partially a response to the previous factor?); the wrong personality for the occupation.

9. Assessment of Staffing Needs: Current Practice

The major aim of this report was to provide an alternative or perhaps supplementary technique to help estimate staffing requirements. Given this aim, it seemed highly relevant to explore how staffing needs were currently assessed (by what means or methods) and how satisfactorily. Within this context, what was the extent of familiarity with and acceptance of the idea of staff to user ratios as an aid to setting staffing levels? The next three subsections examine these themes and the relevant evidence emerging from this study.

9.1 How satisfactory are current methods?

Respondents were asked how staffing needs were estimated for their unit and whether this method worked well in practice. Results (as shown in Table 42, p.70) revealed that the situation might be in need of improvement. The ideal method would not yet seem to be in general use. Relatively few respondents (14%) gave wholehearted support to current methods. They were greatly outnumbered by the 43% who completely disapproved of current methods. Significance tests were carried out on the raw figures on which Table 42 was based. Only the analysis by geographical area failed to reveal significant differences. Siting of service was not an influential factor in this context. Any apparent differences between North, Midlands and South are attributable to chance. Significant differences did emerge however in all the other cross-sorts. Size (significant) and type (highly significant) were factors relating to unit heads' opinion of the staffing level assessment methods used.

The kind of unit most hostile to, or suffering most under, present assessment methods would appear to be: located in a medium-sized organisation; a government service; called a library; in the medical field.

Those most satisfied with current procedures would seem to be: serving a small parent organisation; society or association based; called an information service or by some quite "different" title; non-medical in subject field.

9.2 What methods are used?

Detailed examination of methods used to determine staffing needs makes dissatisfaction seem quite a reasonable reaction to some of them. Various unsatisfactory situations were uncovered in which the head of the library-information unit was deliberately excluded, or given insufficient say in the

Table 42 Reaction to own[1] method of assessing staff requirements

	Base[2] (100%)	Warm (approval, praise) %	Lukewarm (acceptance, toleration) %	Cool (Non-commital or mixed reaction) %	Cold (criticism, disapproval) %
Whole sample	655	94(14%)	184(28%)	95(15%)	282(43%)
Area					
North	144	10	28	13	49
Midlands	88	21	23	14	42
South	423	14	29	15	41
Parent organisation					
Mini	106	13	27	20	40
Small	151	21	32	14	33
Medium	225	11	26	14	49
Large	147	16	27	9	48
Size unknown	26	4	31	31	34
Type					
Industry, Commerce	277	16	34	12	38
Government, etc.	242	10	21	14	55
Society, other	136	19	28	20	33
Service title					
Library	327	13	24	16	47
Information	52	14	42	19	25
Combined	238	13	31	11	45
Different	38	31	29	16	24
Medical v rest					
Medical	128	11	18	23	48
Non-medical	527	15	31	12	42

[1] The word "own" is here used rather loosely, describing methods used by own organisation for library-information service. In fact, such decisions are frequently made at a management level higher than that of the unit head (see also table 43).
[2] Percentages run horizontally.

decision-making process. These included: cases where "higher" management made all decisions; cases where the unit head's opinion was not sought at all; where visiting "experts" decided staffing needs (e.g. consultants, inspectors); where the people doing the assessing were basically very ignorant about the nature of library-information work.

More positive approaches described included: workload analysis; demand related staffing; stock related assessment; research or statistics based methods. The full range of answers given is shown in Table 43. The standard cross analyses are not however provided. A table of this size and complexity is not very amenable to cross-analysis display, nor to testing for significance. Noticeable differences between sub-groups of the sample are however commented on textually.

Table 43 Assessing staff requirements: methods and determinants

655 (100%)	Base
197 (30%)	Central management makes assessment and any decisions arising (includes staff levels set by Personnel Department).
166 (25%)	Financial and economic pressures are the real deciding factors: staff levels are budget controlled or constrained to "what we can afford" rather than "what we need".
156 (24%)	Workload analysis: task related methods, volume of material handled, work volume translated into manhours, etc.
146 (22%)	Demand related: user demand and/or apparent need levels; number of enquiries, loans, etc.
122 (19%)	Service objectives, provision and planning determined: decide what you are going to do, then staff to run that kind of service. This is a positive, but slightly dictatorial approach as opposed to the previous two passive, reactive approaches. It is not necessarily viewed as good, because it can be deliberately perverted to provide minimum service.
108 (16%)	Overtime, over-work and backlog as indicators: when service reaches a certain critical and demonstrable stress point, additional staff are grudgingly appointed.
108 (16%)	Past experience is the decision base and guide: educated guesswork, intuitive evaluation of situations, tradition – includes the belief that staff too small for formal methods to be necessary.
104 (16%)	Unit head has little say in or influence on decisions made, also has little knowledge of methods used or how staff levels are set.
98 (15%)	"Grew like Topsy" and really never has been assessed: arbitrary or ad hoc decision-making; "there is no method or policy".
61 (9%)	Assessment is done by people ignorant about the nature of library-information work and inexperienced in its application or execution.
61 (9%)	Contract, external business, product line related: staffing levels are linked to and reflect organisation's programme of activity and "how business is doing".
57 (9%)	Statistics or research based: systematic data collection and/or active ad hoc research is carried out to establish needs, anticipate trends and back-up staffing demands made by unit head.

(Continued over)

Table 43 *Continued*

655 (100%)	Base
56 (9%)	Fixed establishment rules and standards exist – one works within this framework – e.g. Civil Service, Teaching Hospitals. Overall manning levels for whole organisation may exert indirect control.
39 (6%)	Opening hours determinant: a minimal mechanistic approach – the philosophy behind it is (just) enough staff to keep the service open so many days per week/hours per day.
33 (5%)	Staff to user ratios are in current use.
32 (5%)	Outside experts make all assessments: the organisation invites or is subject to visiting consultants, inspectors, review committees, etc.
28 (4%)	Stock related: staff numbers are closely related to stock size and growth (another physical measure which leaves the user relatively out of account).
24 (4%)	Political and policy pressures as determinants and over-rides.
22 (3%)	Ratios other than staff to user are employed (instead or as well) – e.g. number of loans, departments served, subject areas covered.
21 (3%)	Gaps between theory and practice exist: decisions made do not reflect official assessment results or policies.
14 (2%)	Physical expansion limits, space considerations, accommodation available.
13 (2%)	Any quantification (like ratios, or workload analysis) needs to be related to time (periods), otherwise it is meaningless.
8 (1%)	Comparison with (staffing levels of library-information units in) other "similar" organisations.

Note: Multiple answers were possible. Sometimes more than one method was used in combination, and/or more than one factor acted as an influence. Answer totals therefore exceed the 100% base.

The larger the parent organisation, the more likely it was that central management took the real staffing decisions out of the hands of the unit head. A steady progression of this trend or tendency was shown (whole sample 30%: mini organisations 26%; small 29%; medium 32%; large 33%). Information units were least likely to have decisions made for them by central management (information 17%, cf. 30% for libraries).

Financial and economic pressures were more likely to call the real tune in medical (30%) than non-medical services (24%).

Information services (38%) were the most likely to use workload analysis as a measure of staffing needs. Medical services (16%) were markedly less likely to use workload analysis than non-medical services (26%).

Demand related staffing was less used in minute organisations (15%) than in large ones (27%). Information and "differently" titled services showed an above average reliance on demand related methods (31% and 32% respectively).

The positive future planning and service related approach was low (9%) in minute organisations cf. large ones (24%). It was higher in industry-commerce (23%) than in government (15%) or society (16%) services. Only 13% of libraries cf. 33% of information units adopted the forward planning approach.

Staff stress and work backlog as an indicator was less prevalent in the North (10%) than in the Midlands (20%) or South (18%). It was more prevalent in medical (22%) than non-medical (15%) services.

Heads of society and association services and of information units had an above average say in decisions affecting staffing levels. Only 7% of societies-associations mentioned exclusion, and only 10% of information unit heads. The average for the sample as a whole was 16% mentioning exclusion or "no say". In libraries the exclusion level was 18%.

The library (20%) was much more likely to have "just grown like Topsy" than the information service (8%). The medical service (25%) was more likely than the non-medical one (13%) to have developed in this ad hoc unplanned way.

The larger the service the more prevalent was the feeling that higher management and outside expert decision makers were interfering ignoramuses in library-information terms. The society "librarian" was particularly unlikely to hold this view (3%).

Assessment by complete outsiders (visiting "experts") was rare in industrial-commercial circles (1% mentioned), most commonly cited in government circles (11%).

Societies and associations (12%) and information units (15%) were most likely to use systematically collected background data or to do special research when making a case for more staff.

Fixed establishment rules about staffing were most frequently mentioned by government (15%) and medical (10%) services, least cited by societies and associations (3%).

9.3 Any usage of ratio methods?

First-hand familiarity with user ratio methods was tested by asking respondents if they used or had ever used "any ratios of this general kind when assessing library-information staff requirements or levels". The great majority had never done so. Results for the sample as a whole are shown in Table 44.

Table 44   Use staffing ratios?

655 (100%)	Base
533 (81%)	No never
83 (13%)	Not now, have done in past
33 (5%)	Yes, we do so currently
6 (1%)	Not yet (but plan to do so)

Variation in response was not great between the sub-groups of the sample. Considering this finding and the disparate sizes of the answer groups for the sample as a whole, results were not tested for significance. In any case this could only have been attempted by setting "no never" answers against all other answers combined onto a single group – i.e. presumed unfamiliarity against some degree of first-hand familiarity. Frankly this did not seem a worthwhile or productive exercise.

The fact that in this sample the group who had used some form of ratio assessment in the past and discarded it exceeded the size of the group using or planning to use the method is somewhat perturbing. But then prior to this report there was not very much data collated or available for the "special" field from which to construct, set or establish such ratios. Nevertheless, this point merits examination. What, for instance, were the ratios used by the 18% with practical experience? What was the nature of this experience and the opinion of those using ratios? Why was the ratio method abandoned in some cases? If in fact it was discarded. The respondent may have simply moved on to another job in another organisation where the ratio method was not used or favoured by higher management. How did the large group who had never used ratios react to the idea of this method of assessing staffing requirements? Were any valid objections raised?

Some evidence did emerge from questionnaire results which illuminates, if it does not positively settle, these queries.

Amongst respondents who did or had used staff to user ratios as standards of some kind, the mean average of ratios cited was 1:85 for the sample as a whole. The median was 1:39 and the mode about 1:35. The range of ratios mentioned was large, from 1:9 to 1:856 in one (atypical in this context) government service.

Between the organisational sub-groups of the sample there was marked difference. Mean average ratio for industry-commerce was 1:40, government 1:125, society etc. 1:52.

In quoting these ratios it was clear in most cases that respondents were talking about actual (rather than potential) users and about direct responsibility populations. This gives rise to a few interesting speculations. With the library-information community at large, over the years, some myth-like concept of an ideal ratio of 1:30 seems to have developed. Like most myths, its origins are shrouded in deepest mystery, but repetition seems to have lent it a certain authority. When the subject of staffing and user populations is raised, this ratio will sooner or later be cited by somebody.

Perhaps it arose purely by analogy with the teacher-pupil ideal ratio advocated by educationalists (but seldom achieved in the actual classroom). Librarians in particular, do seem to identify with teachers. Anyway, whatever the cause, there is a tendency to think of 1:30 as an unproven desirable standard.

The embarrassing and crucial question however is: one to thirty-what? This remains somewhat undefined and hazy. Are these people talking about actual or potential users? Or don't they know or have they never thought what they are talking about? It would seem that they are most likely to be talking about potential users, because this is the easier firm population definition from a forward planning point of view. Our respondents who had used ratios however, appeared to base them on actual users (registered borrowers, enquiries recorded by name etc).

It was also interesting to compare actual ratios in force in units that cited ratios as standards. The former were invariably higher than the latter (i.e. more users per staff member). This may be an instance of one of those gaps between policy and actual staffing practice mentioned by respondents (see Tables 43 and 45). On the other hand, an inherent defect of any ratio system may be emerging here. Unless staffing levels in the whole organisation and definitions of potential users are constantly monitored and updated, library-information staffing on a ratio basis may be always lagging behind an expanding reality. Rather like pay claims based on the current cost of living or rate of inflation: by the time increases are awarded, cost of living and inflation have already risen past this level and will continue to do so until the next pay claim and settlement (which once again will be retrospectively oriented).

A retrospectively oriented defect is not however necessarily inherent in the ratio system per se. Extrapolative use of ratios to set forward looking or future library-information staff targets is possible – provided that the parent organisation creates the data on which to base such ratios. If the organisation goes in for company manpower planning and forecasting in a systematic fashion, if it tries to forsee its own future nature, shape and size over the coming years, then the library-information service can also have future based user ratios and can go in for future systems planning. Not only the possible sensible size of the library-information service can be seen, but very probably additional pointers concerning desirable future composition and staff skills will emerge. If for instance, the company (or other organisation) forsees a need, over the next five years, to increase or reduce staff, not only generally but particularly within certain departments, this has repercussions for the kind of expertise needed in the library-information department over that period.

Purists may say that this last made point is technically outside the sphere of a ratio method. I am not so sure. Certainly such factors should be taken into account when using a ratio method. As some of our respondents said: you can't use ratio data in absolute isolation from the other information available to you and hope to solve all your problems.

This issue of access to company forecasting and planning information also underlines the real need for library-information unit heads to be more involved in (or at least aware of) company policy decisions and future plans. If library-information managers are not fully involved or informed, the service provided will always be a reactive, time-lagged, retrospectively oriented one. It will be out of synchronisation with the actualities of company progress, because it is based on outdated experience and guesswork. This applies not only to the number of library-information staff employed, but also to staff nature, composition and subject expertise.

What, however, was the general reaction of our sample to the idea of using ratios as staffing guides? Those clearly in favour (17%) marginally outweighed those clearly opposed (11%). The majority (72%) however had no fixed opinion, or showed a very mixed reaction, in which pros and cons were debated without a definite attitudinal stand being taken. This is hardly surprising. No actual question like: "what do you think of the idea of ratios" was ever put to respondents. This was a deliberate omission, made on the (correct) assumption that most people would be unfamiliar with ratio use, and the principle that it is unfair and often unwise to ask people to describe how they like what they have yet to experience.

However, we did get a fair amount of gratuitous information or comment. Specific doubts or objections were raised by 51% of the sample, 49% raised no objections. This does not however contradict previous statements. Nor is it to be interpreted as 49% clearly in favour. Actually the non-objecting group breaks down into 17% in favour and 32% unable to comment much or clearly define their attitude at all. The group making negative noises similarly breaks down into 11% definitely opposed and 40% with a mixed attitude, citing pros as well as cons.

What were the doubts voiced about use of ratios by 51% of the sample? These ranged from quite serious objections from organisations with large and far-flung potential user populations, to small queries that almost amounted to grudging or mild praise.

Table 45 Specific negative comments on ratio method

655 (100%)	Base
121 (18%)	Difficulty or impossibility of assessing size of whole potential user group: large populations involved, problem of external users.
142 (22%)	Difficulty or impossibility of assessing size of actual user group – either in whole or in part.
63 (10%)	Our organisation and/or unit is too small for (such or any) formal assessment measures to be necessary. Ad hoc methods are adequate, staffing needs show up quickly.
28 (4%)	Potential user numbers are a poor guide to actual usage, little real relationship exists between the two. So ratios are not valid predictors or assessment measures.
30 (5%)	External factors influence usage volume heavily. Usage is more related to the "volume of company business" than to size of the (fairly) static potential user population.
27 (4%)	Internal factors (like the nature and quality of the service provided) influence usage level more than size of population to be served: usage level is a reactive phenomenon, heavily library-information service determined.
2 (0%)	Time periods need to be taken into account: ratios need to be related to this, if used.
25 (4%)	Ratios are useful as one measure among several. "A rough guide no more". They should never be used in isolation, or as the sole indicator of staffing requirements.
22 (3%)	Prone to abuse. Gaps between theory and practice occur. Where ratios are officially used, the real decisions about staffing are seldom based on them.
29 (4%)	Useless to us at the moment. But could conceivably be useful to us in the future (if things change around here).

* Percentages are based on the whole sample, rather than the 51% who voiced dissent, to avoid giving an exaggerated impression of the prevalence of any opinion amongst the sample.

10. Users in General

10.1 Actual, potential and theoretically possible users

What do we really mean when we talk about "users"? Already we have seen that the term library-information "staff" is ambiguous, capable of different interpretations, which need definition before staff to user ratios can be calculated or used. Does, for instance, the term staff include support staff? If so, how are they defined? Does it distinguish between professional and non-professional workers? If so, is the distinction based on post held or qualifications possessed?

The term "user" is similarly capable of multiple interpretation. Does it mean those people who actually avail themselves of the services of the library-information unit? This group I have called the actual users. Or does it mean those who reasonably might be expected to use the service, those groups that the unit was designed or now aims to serve. This definition ignores the question of actual usage and embraces a larger group, including people who for one reason or another are in practice non-users. This group I have called the potential users.

As a library-information unit exists within a given framework — e.g. in the case of the industrial-commercial firm, the whole parent organisation — there is an even larger group of people which could find its way to the service and make demands on it. This group I have called the possible or theoretically relevant population, or to put it less pompously, the total payroll base.

In calculating ratios, these three concentric user groups have been distinguished. Staff to user ratios are provided for each group. Readers and practitioners must decide for themselves which categorisation or definition of user is most relevant to their situation, or most useful to them, in determining the staffing needs of their service.

This decision may also be heavily influenced by the type of information most readily and reliably available to the library-information manager.

In this context some comment on the relevance of the total theoretical population to library-information staffing needs may be appropriate. Readers may be wondering why this categorisation was ever considered by this report and whether it has any relevance at all. Challengers (from Chris Hanson onwards) have queried whether the total size of the parent organisation had any relationship to size of actual user group or of library-information staff. The (usually ad hoc and intuitive) conclusions reached were that no such relationship existed and that size of organisation was no basis on which to assess necessary size of information unit. Admittedly, on an overall basis (library-information units of all kinds) this is sound reasoning, because different types of parent organisation differ in "top-heavyness", intellectual labour-intensity or ratio of Chiefs to Indians on the total payroll.

In this report however, we are restricting ourselves to one broad variety of library-information unit – those within the "special" sector. Within this sector we also distinguish between different kinds of special service in our standard sub-groups or cross-analyses. So "total payroll" did seem worth exploration. Because if there is any relationship, total size would be a very useful base. Total payroll size is the easiest figure to acquire and work with – particularly in the case of projected or newly established services, who are in the process of defining potential users and can have no data as yet on actual usage.

Table 46 Relationship between actual, potential and total possible users (onsite population only)

	Total onsite payroll* (100%)	Potential users			Actual users		
		Av. No. per unit	% of total payroll		Av. No. per unit	% of total payroll	% of potential users
Whole sample	1390	703	(51%)		291	(21%)	(41%)
Area							
North	1031	528	(51%)		263	(26%)	(50%)
Midlands	1926	528	(27%)		252	(13%)	(48%)
South	1392	800	(57%)		307	(22%)	(38%)
Type							
Industry, Commerce	1181	471	(40%)		217	(18%)	(46%)
Government	2191	1265	(58%)		497	(23%)	(39%)
Society, other	322	180	(56%)		88	(27%)	(49%)
Service title							
Library	1896	973	(51%)		365	(19%)	(38%)
Information	502	297	(59%)		115	(23%)	(39%)
Combined	1058	509	(48%)		258	(24%)	(51%)
Different	684	291	(43%)		138	(20%)	(47%)
Medical v rest							
Medical	2346	1218	(52%)		595	(25%)	(49%)
Non-medical	1184	592	(50%)		226	(19%)	(38%)

* Average per organisation or library-information unit

Examining the data provided by our sample, does any mathematical pattern, progression or relationship show up, between total population, potential users and actual users? If so, prediction might be possible on a total population basis.

In fact there did seem to be a crude mathematical progression or doubling up (or halfing down) trend. Potential users represented about half the total payroll. Actual users represented about half the potential user population, or a quarter of the total payroll. Obviously there was variation between the sub-groups of the sample, doubtless dependent on their "boffin or skilled manpower intensivity" or Chiefs to Indians ratio.

Potential users expressed as a percentage of total payroll, for instance, ranged from about 30–60%, depending on the type of organisation. A modal average might be taken as 45%, the mean was 51%. Actual users expressed as a percentage of total payroll ranged from 13–30%. A modal average might be 25%, the mean was 21%. Actual users expressed as a percentage of potential ranged from 40–50%. A modal average might be 45%, the mean was 41%. These comments and the table on which they are based (Table 46) refer only to the onsite user population.

Onsite and offsite user groups are more fully explored in the next section (10.2). The question of mathematical relationships between sectors of the offsite population (a more difficult group to define and measure) is deferred until then (see also tables 48–9).

10.2 Onsite and offsite users

The terms "onsite" and "offsite" represent another dimension of user categorisation, which cuts across the actual, potential, total distinction described in the previous section.

Respondents were asked to describe their potential user populations and to explain how they defined a potential user. An important element in their descriptions was the location of the potential user population.

Onsite users, who worked at or very near to the site of the library-information unit were usually, but not infallibly, employees of the unit's own parent organisation. An exception occasionally encountered was that of the small unrelated organisation, possessing no library facilities of its own, but sharing the same site or building with a larger organisation possessing a library-information service. The informationally-deprived and more astute employees of the small organisation may find their way to the unit and worm or con their way into it. Thus they establish a usage precedent which a kind hearted or democratically minded library-information manager finds it hard to break in future. This points up a distinction between onsite and core or direct responsibility populations. Onsite is not necessarily synonymous with the two last-mentioned categories. Other exceptions include other branches of the organisation possessing no branch "libraries". These may be regarded by the employer as the direct responsibility of the library-information services which do exist within the organisation at other sites. An obvious and numerically significant category is the society or association with its membership. The membership is offsite, but the core target population of most society libraries and information services. So offsite users are a mixed bunch as far as priority rights to library-information service are concerned. The composition of onsite and offsite user groups will be examined in more detail in sections 11 and 12 respectively.

Here it seems more useful to consider the broad composition of potential user groups of different kinds of service, purely in terms of the relative proportions (or mixtures) of onsite and offsite users. From this viewpoint, potential user populations of each service were easy to categorise as composed of: only or mainly onsite people; onsite and offsite in equal (or very substantial) proportions; offsite only or mainly. Distribution within the sub-groups of the sample is shown in Table 47.

The most interesting feature of this table is its demonstration of the general finding that the large majority of services (73%) catered for a mixed onsite-offsite population. A relatively small number of services (15%) were in the "easy" or enviable situation (regarding user predictability) of dealing only or almost exclusively with an onsite user population.

Factors related to siting composition or distribution of user groups were the size of the parent organisation, nature or type of parent organisation, whether the service was medical or not.

Geographical area findings (although provided in Table 47) were not statistically significant (Adjusted $\chi^2 = 4.88$; d.f. $= 4$; p $= 0.30$ approx). Title of service results could not be tested for significance as they stood. The "different" group was too small. A test excluding the "different" name group showed no significant difference between library, information or combined service (Adjusted $\chi^2 = 5.12$; d.f. $= 4$; P $= 0.30$ approx).

To examine differences that were significant: size of parent organisation and onsite-offsite user location were causally related. The typical offsite user oriented organisation was very small in size. The onsite user oriented one was large. This is not really a very surprising finding, but it is a highly significant one – yet another confirmation of the obvious (Adjusted $\chi^2 = 306.04$; d.f. $= 6$; P $= <0.001$).

Table 47 Location of potential users

	Base* (100%)	Onsite only or mainly %	Onsite and offsite %	Offsite only or mainly %
Whole sample	654	96(15%)	477(73%)	81(12%)
Area				
North	144	19	70	11
Midlands	88	14	79	7
South	422	14	72	14
Parent organisation				
Mini	106	10	30	60
Small	151	13	83	4
Medium	225	20	80	—
Large	147	12	88	—
Size unknown	25	16	36	48
Type				
Industry, Commerce	277	20	78	2
Government	242	15	82	3
Society, other	135	3	47	50
Service title				
Library	326	15	70	15
Information	52	13	75	12
Combined	238	14	77	9
Different	38	21	68	11
Medical v rest				
Medical	128	9	84	7
Non-medical	526	16	70	14

* One unit did not supply this information.

An onsite only group was most prevalent in industry and commerce. This again was hardly a revelation. What was surprising was the unexpectedly high proportion of industrial-commercial services possessing mixed onsite-offsite user groups – i.e. coping with outsiders as well as the resident user population (Adjusted $\chi^2 = 227.72$; d.f. = 4; P = <0.001. Differences are highly significant).

Medical services were more likely to be faced with a mixed offsite-onsite user population than non-medical services. At the same time the medical service was less likely than the rest of the sample to deal with a purely onsite or purely offsite group. Remembering the typical hospital library this makes sense. It has responsibility not only for hospital personnel but also for local GP's and area health workers (Adjusted $\chi^2 = 8\cdot08$; d.f. = 2; P = <0·02. Differences are highly significant).

Reverting to the question raised earlier (in section 10.1) about the existence of mathematical relationships between actual and potential user groups, were any patterns observable within offsite populations, or within "whole" populations – i.e. onsite plus offsite? Tables 48 and 49 examine this issue. Readers should note that when dealing with offsite users there is no possible equivalent of the total payroll figure. What would one use? One could be lead into nonsensical areas, giving serious consideration to the population of the United Kingdom (or Europe, or the World) as the total theoretically relevant population. Only actual or potential users can be defined or identified in the offsite context. For this reason the total payroll-type column (as shown in Table 46) is omitted from Tables 48–9.

The general trend in these tables is clear, particularly when compared with that for onsite users in isolation (46). Potential offsite users are numerous. Large groups of people are involved. Yet only a relatively small percentage of these people actually get round to using the relevant services. Perhaps this is merciful, as their huge potential size represents an implicit threat to the average library-information unit. Examining the size of some of these potential external groups, one begins to feel the full force of the fears some librarians express concerning them and concerning particularly the effect of publicising the service: "Don't rock the boat. Don't stir up a demand we can't possibly meet"; "If all the people with an interest in our subject field, or a theoretical right to use this service (even minimally) found their way here – then God help us! We simply could not cope".

So offsite usage can be described as much less intensive and extensive than onsite usage. In the latter case a far higher proportion of potential users do avail themselves of the service. Probably they also do so more often. Perhaps this is because it is relatively easy to use a same-site service. Another instance of information seeking behaviour being very much a matter of taking the path of least resistance or the easiest available option?

Table 48   Relationship between actual and potential users (offsite only)

	Base (100%) Potential Users[1]	Actual Users	
		Av. No per unit	% of potential
Whole sample	24360	1185	(4.9)
Industry, Commerce	4973	397	(8.0)
Government	24161	273	(1.1)
Society[2], etc.	64061	4419	(6.9)

[1] Average number per unit.
[2] Includes other offsite users besides members – e.g. bona fide enquirers

Table 49 Relationship between actual and potential users (offsite plus onsite)

	Base (100%) potential users[1]	Actual users	
		Av. No. per unit	% of potential
Whole sample	25063	1476	(5.9)
Industry, Commerce	5444	614	(11.3)
Government	25426	770	(3.0)
Society, etc[2]	64241	4507	(7.0)

[1] [2] As defined for table 48.

11. Onsite Users

11.1 Broad parameters of potential user definition

"How did you define a potential user? For which departments or staff categories do you consider it your responsibility to provide?" Respondents were asked these questions. Answers were illuminatingly specific in many cases. From them a fairly detailed identikit picture of the potential user group can be built up (see Tables 53–4, which display this material).

At the same time, some deliberately non-specific answers gave the clue to broader-based attitudes and policies on usage underlying some of the more detailed and specific answers. These non-specific answers evinced an extremely democratic and non-discriminatory stand on information provision and "the right to know". On closer examination more detailed answers revealed other stances of various kinds on this issue. They can be arranged in a continuum or scale with a "right to know" or open house pole or policy at one end and a "need to define" (if proper service is to be purposefully given) at the other. This scale is shown in Table 50.

Table 50 Broad definitions of onsite potential users: summary

655 (100%)	Base
187 (28%)	"Anyone on the staff with a need to know".
83 (13%)	Anyone in theory, no-one excluded: but in practice more service is given to or demanded by certain staff categories.
60 (9%)	Nearly everyone, excludes a few categories at bottom of hierarchy – i.e. "all except manual workers".
8 (1%)	Nearly everyone, excludes a few categories on a subject (not covered) basis – e.g. "we don't supply commercial information".
267 (41%)	Target audience is more clearly, tightly defined and restricted group of onsite staff categories (than any of the above).
50 (8%)	Onsite staff are not mentioned as part of the target audience at all.

Information shown in Table 50 could be further summarised from a slightly different viewpoint, with meaningful results. Taking the group of 605 services who catered for onsite staff (either alone or in combination with offsite users), findings can also be described thus: 31% of this group had an open (house) definition of the onsite user (would and/or did serve anybody if necessary); 25% had a fairly loose definition or fairly free and easy access policy; 44% had a much tighter definition and policy.

On the basis of this distinction between open, loose and tight definitions, the standard analyses by the sub-groups of the sample were carried out. No significant differences showed up between the sub-groups, except in the case of medical versus non-medical services. Apparently medical services really were more likely to have a tighter onsite user definition and policy than non-medical services. Adjusted $\chi^2 = 7 \cdot 49$; d.f. = 2; P = <0·03. Differences are significant, bordering on being highly so. Table 51 presents the results of the medical, non-medical analysis. Other sub-group analyses are not presented, for obvious reasons.

Table 51 Broad definitions of onsite potential users

	Whole (relevant) sample	Medical services	Non-medical
Base (100%)	605	120	485
Open-house	187 (31%)	29 (24%)	158 (33%)
Loosely defined	151 (25%)	24 (20%)	127 (26%)
Tightly defined	267 (44%)	67 (56%)	200 (41%)

11.2 Service bias in user definition

Amongst those unit heads (418) who did define their target audience in any way and to any degree, what was the direction of bias, or basis of "discrimination"? The latter term is very applicable here in its dual sense of discriminate against (certain categories of theoretically possible users) and exercise a fine judgment in so doing.

In fact (and once again) a bias scale can be constructed from responses. This is displayed in Table 52, and covers the whole sample.

Attitude and motivation of the unbiased group are worth further exploration. At first superficial examination an impression forms that this is a fine tolerant example of that people-directed approach recommended (but sometimes lacking) in libraries and information services. The managers who said: "I would never turn away anyone who needed information, no matter who they were," sound like (and probably are) nice people. But are they wise managers and good "organisation men"? After all, this is the special sector we are concerned with here, not the public library context.

As we have seen, special library-information services tend to be small in almost every sense – in staff size, limited resources, budget allocation, political power and status within the parent organisation. So service to anyone and everyone may reduce the level of service to people with a more urgent (and organisationally more cogent) need or "right to know". Additionally, the library-information unit may be undermining an already weak position by

Table 52   Service bias re onsite or inhouse potential users

655 (100%)	Base
248 (38%)	*Little detectable bias:* no overt expression or much indication of bias or discrimination (this group consists of 187 "open houses" and 61 of the "loose-definers" or "fairly free and easy" group).
(357 = 54%)	*Selective bias:* Bias is present and overt concerning some classes of inhouse user: direction of bias is:
110 (17%)	hierarchical, status based. The library-information unit exists to serve important people. Service is given above certain grades, "middle management upwards", to "VIP's" etc.
62 (9%)	professional, intellectual. "Graduate" or "professional staff" are thought of as the potential users, often regardless of their discipline.
185 (28%)	discipline, organisational function or subject area oriented. Such parameters are the real determinants, often regardless of the grade of worker. The service covers or caters for certain subject areas only – e.g. "all technical staff", "scientists and technicians", "all medical and para-medical workers".
50 (8%)	*Complete bias:* the service is not *intended* for the use of the organisation's own staff, but for offsite populations – e.g. some membership, or public service organisations, also a few institutions providing an information service in a published format.

indulging in this kind of philanthropy. Obviously and admittedly, nasty things like value judgments and the politics of departmental survival are intruding here. As the parent organisation funds and provides the library-information service, value judgments must necessarily be those implicit in the fundamental aims and targets of the organisation itself.

Maybe a canteen worker or a laboratory assistant does have a need to know and in any sane or humane society a right to know. But is the "firm's library" always the right place to bring this need? The need itself needs examination before this question can be answered. Even if the need is concerned with work, does satisfying the needs of relatively unskilled and "unimportant" contributors to organisational progress and profit do as much for the organisation as helping the management or the scientists, engineers, architects etc (i.e. the specialist staff)?

The last mentioned kind of investment of library-information time and resources is probably more productive in terms of organisational survival and progress. In the long run, it could also be argued that it is likely to be more beneficial to the canteen worker and laboratory assistant, because it contributes (albeit indirectly) to their continued employment and adequate renumeration.

Selective bias, therefore, would seem to be necessary from an organisational point of view. Not only is definition of the user group necessary, but it also needs to be very carefully done. It also requires constant monitoring and updating. Defining the user group is not a one-off initial exercise. Again, monitoring the current relevance of user group definition must be done with organisational aims and development in mind.

At this point, one of the dangers of selective bias – as opposed to a relatively "open house" policy – emerges. If bias is mistakenly applied in wrong directions, or is outdated (right for yesterday, wrong for today), then the organisation might well benefit more from an open-house policy. At least in the latter case no-one of potential organisational "value" is excluded by definition, although the service they receive may be limited because it is spread thin over the entire payroll complement.

So, as it may be impossible to serve everybody properly, the library-information manager needs to think very carefully about groups he can most usefully serve (not groups s/he can serve easily from existing stock, resources or expertise). These groups should be selected on the basis of their contribution, actual and potential, to current and future organisational progress and development. Another instance of the imperative need for library-information managers to be a real part of the management structure – i.e. fully informed of organisational plans, problems and policies.

An allied doubt concerning "open house" library-information systems is also worth airing. In some cases statements about open-house policy sounded very like misplaced liberalism, of the kind implicit in preceding paragraphs. In others, however, it sounded more sinister. Frankly, sometimes it seemed to amount to pseudo-democracy camouflaging ignorance. The head of the service may not have a clue who s/he ought to be serving, nor what the service is supposed to be doing, nor why the unit exists at all. To appear busy and necessary all and sundry may be frantically welcomed. So a useful smoke-screen in terms of departmental survival is set up. It may cover chaos, apathy and organisational ignorance. It is yet another example of the need for full organisational involvement. Total blame certainly should not be laid on the librarian or information manager. The fault is dual. The parent organisation and higher management seem fundamentally to blame, for not making plain what they need and expect from the library-information unit. It is difficult to imagine, for example, a research, production, marketing or sales department left to flounder in this undirected fashion by management. On the other hand, surely the library-information manager is also to blame? S/he could at least try to find out the reason for his/her organisational existence. A lack of simple human curiosity seems to be demonstrated here, amounting to an uncommitted, passive, perhaps fearful or even parasitical apathy.

11.3 Privilege and deprivation: In-groups and out-groups

A valuable spin-off from attempts to collect quantitative data on user numbers was the large amount of information provided which defined and described the user in qualitative terms. In fact we may well have got a rather better idea of the nature of the user (particularly the potential user) population, as a result of this project, than we have of its absolute size.

The question asking respondents how they defined a potential user was positively worded. In other words, basically it asked by implication who would be let in, not who would be shut out. So it is not surprising that a positive presentation was usually chosen as the answer format. Respondents tended to describe the kind of people who were expected to use their services, rather than those who were excluded or not expected to make demands.

"In-group" definition was the norm. Nevertheless by implication, imagination and subtraction, this tells us something about the likely composition of the "out-group". Some respondents did actually define the "out-group", but these results are not worth presentation as a formal table or cross-analysis. Readers may however be interested to know that of the whole sample (655), 2%

Table 53 Potential users: inhouse priority groups

Rank	422(100%)	Base[1]
1	172(41%)	Administrators, management, VIP's
11	29(7%)	Commercial, financial departments
12	22(5%)	Design, art department, draughtsmen drawing office
2	148(35%)	Engineers and technologists (inc. data processing)
12	22(5%)	External and public relations, "soft sell"
9	42(10%)	— "Hard sell": sales, marketing advertising
5	94(22%)	Graduate or professional staff
11	29(7%)	Internal relations and welfare
7	74(18%)	Medical – graduates: physicians and surgeons, pharmacists, dentists, vets
10	36(9%)	— Nurses
9	42(10%)	— Other medical and paramedical
14	7(2%)	— Patients[2]
11	30(7%)	Production, including quality control and analysis
14	9(2%)	Professions of a non-scientific, non-technical nature
3	124(29%)	Research and development
6	83(20%)	Scientists, "scientific staff"
8	48(11%)	Students, apprentices, trainees
11	30(7%)	Support and service – clerical secretarial
15	4(1%)	— Household: catering, grounds, and premises, cleaning
4	113(27%)	— Technicians and scientific support: highly skilled labour
13	13(3%)	— Workshop, blue collar, craftsmen and manual
11	31(7%)	Teachers and trainers, instructors

[1] Lower than usual, because some services have an open-house policy (anybody is a potential user, without discrimination) and some other services do not have an inhouse user population, only an external one. Multiple answers were possible.
[2] This covered information supply to patients, *not* recreational reading.

mentioned administrators as excluded; 5% mentioned clerical and secretarial workers; 1% mentioned those needing financial information (e.g. accounts department); 3% mentioned "household" staff (canteen, cleaners); 1% mentioned maintenance staff; 3% mentioned support staff in general; 1% mentioned "production"; 4% mentioned "blue collar" or shop floor workers; 2% mentioned technicians.

Positive results, describing and defining the "in-group" expected to need or avail themselves of library-information services, are presented in Table 53. As it seemed important to preserve as much as possible of respondents' own terminology and conceptualisation, the list became rather long. Categories are not necessarily mutually exclusive. It may however give a better picture of the way respondents see their potential users, than a shorter list using vague broad all-embracing categories. The list is arranged in alphabetico-classified order. Rank order (based on number of mentions) is also provided.

A full analysis of sub-groups of the sample would be difficult to supply within the confines of the printed page. It would also be unwieldy and confusing to consult from the reader's point of view, even if producible.

Nevertheless it was realised that any differences between different kinds of organisations and service were likely to be of great interest to readers. As there were some differences, a summarised version of main findings for sub-groups has been prepared and is supplied in Table 54.

11.4 Reliability or hardness of onsite numerical data

Discerning readers will be wondering by now about the reliability of quantitative information concerning onsite users (actual, potential and theoretically possible) supplied in this report and by respondents. Did the respondent necessarily know (and if so with what degree of accuracy) the answer to questions on inhouse or onsite user group size?

The problem also troubled me at the planning stage of this project. So, to get some idea of relative hardness (or fuzziness) of numerical data given in answers, respondents were asked to annotate it where necessary with an E for estimate or G for guess. This instruction had the additional purpose of inducing people who did not know the exact precise figure to provide an approximation. Complete "don't knows" from people who really knew well enough the approximate size of the group, but lacked the latest exact figure, seemed highly undesirable loss of valuable information. "Don't know" responses were only desired from people who genuinely had not got a clue.

Another category of imprecision, besides estimate and guess, was spontaneously provided by the respondents themselves. It was "approximate" – a

Table 54 Priority ranking of inhouse potential users: selective sub-group analysis

Rank	N.	(1)	%	(2)	%	(3)	%	(4)	%
Whole sample	(422)	Administrators	(41)	Engineers	(35)	Research	(29)	Technicians	(27)
Area									
North	(107)	Administrators	(41)	Engineers	(38)	Technicians	(32)	Research	(27)
Midlands	(57)	Administrators	(42)	Research	(40)	Technicians & Engineers		Medical Grads.	(25)
South	(258)	Administrators	(42)	Engineers	(34)	Research	(32) (29)	Technicians	(23)
Parent Organisation									
Mini	(56)	Professional & Research	(30)	Administrators	(25)	Engineers	(18)	Technicians	(13)
Small	(107)	Administrators	(40)	Engineers	(34)	Scientists	(32)	Research	(29)
Medium	(153)	Administrators	(45)	Engineers	(43)	Technicians	(31)	Research	(30)
Large	(97)	Administrators	(44)	Engineers	(37)	Research	(31)	Medical Grads. & Technicians	(30)
Size unknown	(9)	—		—		—		—	
Type Industry,									
Commerce	(175)	Engineers	(56)	Administrators	(43)	Research	(42)	Technicians	(33)
Government	(171)	Administrators & Medical Grads	(38)	Scientists	(27)	Professionals	(26)	Technicians	(24)
Society etc.	(76)	Administrators	(39)	Professionals	(29)	Research	(28)	Engineers	(23)
								Scientists	(22)
Service Title									
Library	(212)	Administrators	(39)	Medical Grads.	(27)	Engineers & Technicians	(26)	Research	(24)
Information	(33)	Administrators & Engineers	(39)	Professionals	(30)	Research & Technicians		Sales & Scientists	(24)
Combined	(151)	Administrators	(45)	Engineers	(41)	Research	(27)	Technicians	(26)
Different	(26)	Engineers	(65)	Administrators & Technicians	(35)	Professionals	(31)	Research	(19)
Medical v Rest									
Medical	(100)	Medical Grads.	(72)	Paramedical	(40)	Nurses	(36)	Administrators	(26)
Non-medical	(322)	Administrators	(45)	Engineers	(43)	Research	(34)	Technicians	(27)

Note: Underlining denotes a user-category ranking atypically high in a particular type of service.

rounded figure, cited for official purposes within and by the organisation. As such it must be presumed in most cases to be of a higher order of reliability than respondents' estimates.

The four categories of data reliability we had to work with were: unqualified answer (hard data); approximation (rounded data); estimate; guess. Distribution of these four categories amongst answers concerning total staff complement of the organisation, potential users within the organisation and actual onsite users is shown in Table 55, 56 and 57 respectively.

Table 55   Total payroll data reliability

614 (100%)	Base
396(65%)	Unqualified answer, hard data
134(22%)	Approximation, rounded answer
69(11%)	Estimate
15(2%)	Guess
655(100%)	Base
614(94%)	"Know", to varying extent as defined above
41(6%)	Really don't know, or this information "classified"*

* An answer occasionally received from government services.

So 87% of numerical information received in the context of total payroll complement could be described as reliable, 98% as fairly reliable, only 2% as unreliable.

Even that 2% may have been more accurate or reliable than it seemed. Educated guesses can come close to truth. For those who doubt this assertion, a small example from the author's personal experience is cited. It is not purely anecdotal, dismissable evidence, "generalizing from a sample of one". It could be backed up with other evidence. It was however readily to hand. A full-scale literature search for bibliographically impeccable additional evidence did not seem warranted to hammer home a minor point.

A market research company was interested in the validity of guess answers, wondering whether it was worthwhile to press respondents (who had claimed they did not know the answer to a certain question) to "have a guess". So during a survey on a recently introduced brand of toilet soap, respondents were asked what colour it was. People who put up the "don't know" gambit were encouraged to guess. The guesses paralleled the assured answers, both coming up with the correct colour (a very pale pink) in the majority of cases.

Cynical readers may be thinking that this is no exemplary feat of pure guesswork. Pink is a common colour for toilet soap. White, yellow, blue and green however are also standard soap colours, which broadens the possibility of guessing wrong, if guessing were all that was involved. Another objection raised might be that perhaps colour was implicit in the name of the soap (all part of a unified brand image design). Often this is the case, but it was not so here. Actually the name strongly suggested either an ivory coloured or pure white soap.

Another sample of respondents were not asked to guess colour (when professing ignorance) but were urged to guess the shape of the soap. Answers of the knowledgeably assured again did not differ significantly from those prepared to guess. This provides much more conclusive evidence. Because although the colour fitted into the standard conventional range, the shape certainly did not. It had what might be described as a special design feature, highly unusual at that time.

The conclusion reached as a result of this "experiment" was that many respondents may know more than they think they do, or are prepared to say. It's not so much a matter of not knowing, in a lot of cases, as of not being quite sure and not wanting to look a fool if one is wrong. A "don't know" answer might be as much a reflection of personality and general self-assurance as of a state of knowledge or informedness. If people are prepared to "have a guess", their answers represent acceptable material from the researcher's point of view.

Taking into consideration the low level of guess answer, and fairly low level of "don't know" answer, the data we do have on user group sizes seems usable "of the order of" material (see also Tables 56–7), particularly in the absence of other information or other research on this subject. All that is claimed for this piece of research is pioneering status, an attempt to find some approximate figures and fit them into an aching void. A dental analogy would be the temporary filling.

Examination of analyses of sub-groups of the sample (re total payroll size) indicated that one factor in particular conditioned extent of respondent confidence in accuracy of information supplied. The factor was of course size of parent organisation. Where other factors also seemed to be related it was probably because they themselves are linked to the factor of organisational size in some way. So they indirectly reflect that influence rather than exerting influence in their own right. Arithmetic progression can be observed in some of the sub-sorts. An absolutely exact answer on total payroll size was provided by 91% of minute organisations, 65% of small, 59% of medium-sized and 54% of large ones. The larger the organisation, the harder it must be to know this with perfect accuracy – unless you work in the payroll department itself. Medical services were low on absolute accuracy (45%), but habitually serve large user complexes and parent organisations. Libraries were lower than any other kind of service title (60% assured accuracy of answer). Societies and associations, with typically small onsite organisational structures, had a high level of unqualified assured accuracy of answer on total staff size (79%). They also habitually produce yearbooks citing this kind of figure, which probably also helps.

Table 56 Potential onsite user data reliability

606 (100%)	Base
423 (70)%)	Unqualified answer, hard data
65 (11%)	Approximation, rounded answer
85 (14%)	Estimate
33 (5%)	Guess
655 (100%)	Base
606 (93%)	"Know" to varying extent, as defined above
49 (7%)	Really don't know or unwilling to reveal

Information provided about the onsite potential user population is examined from the point of view of reliability in Table 56. Respondents' confidence in reliability of the data they provided did not correlate with size of parent organisation (as it did in the case of total payroll data). It is curious and perhaps slightly alarming that the levels of estimate and guess in this context were higher than those relating to payroll data. The level of hard data is however also higher. What is lower here is the "approximate" answer.

Table 57 Actual onsite user data reliability

588 (100%)	Base
309 (53%)	Unqualified answer, hard data
95 (16%)	Approximation, rounded answer
102 (17%)	Estimate
82 (14%)	Guess
655 (100%)	Base
588 (90%)	"Know" to varying extent, as defined above
67 (10%)	Really don't know or unwilling to reveal

A progressive negative correlation between size of parent organisation and supply of "hard" data was again evident in the context of actual onsite usage. The following selective results indicate the trend.

Unqualified, hard data answers: mini 84%; small 64%; medium 49%; large organisations 29%.

Guesses: mini 5%; small 5%; medium 17%; large 23%.

As the large parent organisation obviously contributed more heavily to the data pool on which in-house or onsite ratios were based, this detailed finding gives cause for concern. The comparative unreliability or more approximate nature of data large organisations felt able to supply must be a heavier source of error than the number of units or services involved in this "large" category would indicate. This defect must be admitted by the author and understood by readers.

In defence one can only say that this report did not and could not (with the time, staff and funds made available) research all the user and potential user data personally and with fine accuracy. It has never claimed to do so, nor to provide the final accurate answer and the absolute ratios. It did aim to do a pioneering job, and would claim that it has fairly done so. In the complete absence of any fully and exhaustively research data or standards for the special sector, its results may prove useful as guidelines to practitioners.

As an analytical chemist once said to me (in the course of a survey): "Even dubious data can be immensely useful. In the complete absence of critically evaluated data, *any* research results with which to compare my own findings or experience, are of value". Many library-information managers may feel themselves currently in the same situation as that chemist. So they may find this report, for a time and in the absence of anything better, to be of some practical use.

12. Offsite Users

Offsite usage is a complex phenomenon. It represents a mix of many user types and needs and of degree and nature of service responsibility for or "charity" shown towards users from without the parent organisation.

User types which spring most readily to mind in the context of offsite usage are probably the member and the bona fide user. These two categories alone are illustrative of variation in extent of responsibility for different kinds of offsite user. The membership is an elite priority group, frequently considered to be more "important" than the parent organisation's own staff. The bona fide user in an object of intellectual charity, or perhaps a potential member and so not to be completely dismissed or alienated by refusal of any assistance.

Many other types of offsite user however exist. As we have already seen (in section 10.2), only 15% of the sample had no offsite users or almost negligeable offsite use. These other categories of outside user are described in section 12.2 after examination of member users in 12.1.

12.1 Members and subscribers

Eighteen percent of our sample (115 institutions) had members or subscribers, 82% did not. The typical membership organisation was small, in terms of its own staff or total payroll size. So library–information staff efforts here were of necessity outer-directed. A tendency that is in any case reinforced by a prevalent value judgment that members have priority service rights over inhouse staff, should any conflict arise about available time or resources.

Generally, but not invariably, the membership organisation was a society or association, or some other kind of learned or professional institution. However, 26% of societies and associations did not have a closed or formal membership, whereas 3% of industrial–commercial organisations and 3% of government establishments did have what amounted to a membership – i.e. regular clients, subscribers to a bought service of some kind, or other externals with a recognised right to use various services provided by the institution, including the library–information service.

A membership represents a particularly difficult user body with which to cope. It can be such a far flung and scattered offsite population. Ratio tables have already demonstrated the difficulty of estimating actual usage amongst members (see section 4). The membership may include overseas people. In fact it seems more usual for it to do so than to be confined to the United

Kingdom alone. Admittedly sheer distance should diminish usage frequency amongst overseas members. Nevertheless, postal enquiries are easily made, but not necessarily so easily answered. Problems of language, social, cultural, industrial, economic, even legislative differences between countries may make overseas enquiries tricky to handle.

Table 58 Membership organisations

655 (100%)	Base
39 (6%)	United Kingdom members only
73 (11%)	UK and Overseas members
1 (0%)	Overseas members only
2 (0%)	Members not defined geographically
540 (82%)	No members

Whether membership was on a corporate or individual basis was felt to be relevant information. A corporate membership places a potentially heavier load on the library-information service than a membership composed of individuals. One digit in the corporate membership figures can stand for any number of hidden potential users behind the scenes who may at any stage erupt into active enquiry, either on their own behalf or via their librarian information officer or society representative. It was impossible in constructing the ratios to estimate, weight or allow for this aspect of corporate membership. Readers may however care to bear this in mind when looking at society offsite user figures. In some cases, the one stands for many. It may be useful to know the extent of corporate membership within our sample.

Amongst the 115 membership organisations, 34 (29%) had only or mainly corporate memberships, 71 (62%) had only or mainly individual memberships, 10 (9%) had memberships composed of a roughly equal mix of corporate bodies and individuals.

12.2 Any other offsite users?

Besides onsite employees and offsite members, organisations often assume some responsibility for information and document supply to other offsite groups. Amongst our sample this practice was so widespread that the onsite user group began to look like the mere tip of the iceberg, as far as potential library-information workload was concerned (see Table 59).

Only 14% of the sample said that they did not have any "other" offsite users. Other offsite users include two categories not previously examined. The *bona fide enquirer* belongs here. This type of user is often helped. Twenty six percent of our sample mentioned the bona fide user as a substantial component of their user population. The services concerned were not just societies or associations but included industrial-commercial and government units.

The kind and amount of assistance given to the bona fide enquirer is however variable from service to service. It may be very deliberately rationed. Such restriction may be in terms of input of staff time and effort to enquiries from this source (protection of staff time). Or it may affect the extent to which bona fide users are permitted to avail themselves of self-help facilities normally extended to the core user population. Bona fide users may be allowed to consult documents on the premises, for example, but may not borrow them (protection of stock).

The ultimate aim, of course, of protecting both available labour, or staff-time and stock is protection of the rights of the core user (seen as the library-information unit's real responsibility). There is another type of offsite user, however, who does have priority rights over the bona fide enquirer and who does count as part of the direct responsibility population of the library-information unit. This our man (or woman) in Havana, Paris or Potters Bar – the *offsite employee of the parent organisation*. As well as nomadic members of the sales force, field workers, surveyors, overseas executives, etc "other branches of the firm" were cited in this context. If these branches have no library-information units of their own, or only a minimally and non-professionally staffed document collection, they are likely to make heavy demands on any other branch of the firm possessing an organised service. Their needs will also be accepted as the direct responsibility of any existing formal services. Branch libraries, as well as branch offices without libraries, may also request this kind of help from head office libraries. Respondents mentioned "other librarians and information officers" as part of their offsite user group. The issue here becomes somewhat confusing however. Some of these other librarians and information officers work for other parent organisations and so really belong with or should be regarded as part of the bona fide population. The "help" given here is also part of a give and take, two-way process. Library-information workers often contacted one another in such a way, by mutual agreement. The degree of formality and structuring of such arrangements ranged from loose old-boy, friendly networks to formal inter-library co-operation or information exchange schemes for defined geographical areas, industries, and occupational or functional groups.

Material provided by respondents in response to questions about other offsite users is presented in Tables 59–61. Extent of the offsite user phenomenon is broadly shown in Table 59. Detailed categories or types of other offsite user are described in Tables 60–61. In Table 59 only the organisational type cross sort is provided, as results for the other cross sorts did not differ significantly. Type of organisation apparently is the only factor related to possession of external user groups other than members. Adjusted $\chi^2 = 8.64$; d.f. = 2; $P = 0.02$. Differences are highly significant.

Table 59 Any other outside users (besides members)

	Base (100%)	Yes	No
WHOLE SAMPLE	655	561(86%)	94(14%)
Industry, Commerce	277	224(81%)	53(19%)
Government, etc	242	213(88%)	29(12%)
Society, other	136	124(91%)	12(9%)

Table 60 Composition of other offsite user groups

655 (100%)	Base*
235 (36%)	Own organisation's offsite users: subsidiaries, branches or divisions etc., located elsewhere.
172 (26%)	Bona fide enquirers, scholars, researchers, people with justification to know.
118 (18%)	Medical and paramedical personnel. Doctors, dentists, veterinarians, nurses, pharmacists, "all NHS staff in the area," etc.
117 (18%)	Adult education: academic staff and students.
101 (15%)	Other librarians and information workers on a casual informal basis: the old boy (old girl?) network.
99 (15%)	Industrial and commercial firms.
73 (11%)	Overseas based people (may be own organisation, associate companies, or bona fide status).
70 (11%)	Co-operative information exchange schemes (library-information or industrial), formal.
66 (10%)	Government departments or personnel (includes Armed Forces and nationalised industry).
60 (9%)	Customers, clients, contractors, readers, subscribers other than members, course attenders.
51 (8%)	General public: anyone with a need to know or interest in the area covered by the service: "almost impossible to define".
48 (7%)	Learned societies, research associations.
36 (5%)	Local authorities (other than public libraries).
34 (5%)	Laboratories, scientific and technical establishments.
27 (4%)	Other organisations sharing the same site or building (propinquity and opportunism) and visiting experts/expert "temps".
18 (3%)	Secondary education (sense of responsibility to the young): school children, teachers, parents.
14 (2%)	Media: press, radio, TV, etc.
9 (1%)	Ex-staff members of the organisation (and the corollary – "Libraries and places where I used to work").

* On balance it seemed more meaningful to percentage on the base of the whole sample rather than that of the 561 units with such offsite users.

In the case of table 60 it is impossible to present a full cross-analysis by sub-groups. So a selective presentation of main differences within the sample is provided in table 61.

Table 61 Composition of other offsite user groups: selective sub-group analysis

Rank	N	(1)	%	(2)	%	Top four categories* (3)	%	(4)	%
Whole Sample	(655)	Own offsite	(36)	Bona fide	(26)	Medical	(18)	Lib-inf. casual	(15)
						Academic	(18)	Firms	(15)
Area									
North	(144)	Own offsite	(32)	Academic & Medical		Bona fide	(20)	Lib-inf. casual	(13)
Midlands	(88)	Own offsite	(43)	Medical	(21)	Bona fide	(20)	Academic	(19)
South	(423)	Own offsite	(36)	Bona fide	(24)	Firms & Academic	(17)	Medical	(16)
					(24)				
Parent Organisation									
Mini	(106)	<u>Bona fide</u>		Academic	(24)	Own offsite & Public	(17)	Societies & Overseas	(14)
Small	(151)	Own offsite	(36)	Bona fide	(25)	Academic	(23)	Firms & Lib-inf. casual	(17)
Medium	(225)	Own offsite	(39)	Bona fide	(21)	Medical	(18)	Firms	(16)
Large	(147)	Own offsite	(50)	Medical	(28)	Lib-inf. casual	(22)	Firms	(19)
Type									
Industry, Commerce	(277)	Own offsite	(54)	<u>Firms</u>	(18)	<u>Co-op schemes; Lib-inf. casual & Overseas</u>	(16)	Bona fide	(13)
Government	(242)	<u>Medical</u>	(37)	Own offsite	(31)	Bona fide	(23)	Academic	(20)
Society	(136)	<u>Bona fide</u>	(42)	Academic	(33)	Societies	(18)	Public	(15)
Service Title									
Library	(327)	Own offsite	(29)	Medical	(26)	Bona fide	(24)	Academic	(23)
Information	(52)	Own offsite	(42)	Bona fide & Clients	(25)	Overseas	(21)	Firms	(19)
Combined Different	(238)	Own offsite	(44)	Bona fide	(19)	Lib-inf. casual	(17)	Firms	(16)
	(38)								
Medical v Rest									
Medical	(218)	<u>Medical</u>	(81)	Own offsite	(27)	Lib-inf. casual	(16)	<u>Local authority</u>	(15)
Non-medical	(527)	Own offsite	(38)	Bona fide	(25)	Academic & Firms	(18)	Lib-inf. casual	(15)

* Measured purely in terms of number of units possessing this type of offsite user. Does not necessarily represent the size of the user

12.3 Reliability or representativeness of data on other offsite usage

Membership information was well and confidently quantified by most relevant organisations, as far as potential usage (i.e. whole membership) was concerned. This kind of information is readily available, not only within such organisations, but in published yearbooks. In cases where figures were not given by respondents it appeared that they were deliberately withholding the information as classified, rather than existing in a state of personal ignorance. Among the 115 membership organisations, 12 (10%) did not fully quantify membership.

Actual users within the membership could be much more difficult to identify and quantify, depending on whether records like "borrowers' registers" were kept or library tickets issued. But again statistics which help answer such questions were often automatically kept by membership organisations, for inclusion in yearbook reports on the activities of departments. Among the membership organisations 23 (20%) were unable or unwilling to quantify the size of the actual user group.

Numbers of other offsite users were however poorly or sketchily quantified. Respondents were slightly better able to quantify actual user populations than potential ones. In practice the potential population can sometimes be impossible to quantify, as the following quotation indicates.

"Anyone in the country, or even the world, with an interest in our subject field might conceivably want to consult us at some time. How do you begin to estimate this?"

In the case of potential offsite users (other than members) out of the whole sample of 655 units: 14% had no such users; 57% had such users but were unable to properly quantify or even estimate their numbers; 29% provided useable quantitative data. Very probably these units who were able to do so were atypical by virtue of the very fact that they could quantify. Smaller potential populations and more defined ones seem likely to have been involved.

A very real problem or dilemna is emerging here. Reliable ratios can only be provided or calculated for direct responsibility populations – i.e. onsite and membership. Yet all the indications are that this only represents the tip of the user population iceberg for the average special librarian. To really assess staffing needs more quantitative information about outside users other than members is badly needed. By its very nature, however, it seems almost impossible to acquire in the majority of cases.

13. Outreach and Non-Routine Services

Respondents were asked whether they provided any extra services to users. This question did not specifically include mechanisation, on-line search facilities etc. This topic was reserved for special separate consideration in a series of subsequent questions. Some of the non-routine services mentioned may have used computers or word-processors as adjuncts. Comparison between Table 62 (non-routine service provision) and Table 66 (computer usage) is relevant in this context.

Returning to the question of other outreach or non-routine service provision, the majority of units in our sample (91%) did provide something of this nature. Specific facilities cited, however, tended to be basic and simple (e.g. journal circulation) and/or conventional and familiar (current awareness, SDI). More unusual, ingenious, expertise stretching services were also mentioned, but far less frequently. Detailed findings are presented in Table 62.

Table 62   Provision of non-routine services

655 (100%)	Base
61 (9%)	No provision
594 (91%)	Some provision (details below)*
466 (71%)	Journal circulation (including contents pages only).
440 (67%)	Current awareness service.
362 (55%)	Selective dissemination of information (SDI): indications that can be rudimentary in some cases – e.g. manual (visual!) scan with individual's interests in mind, then fed to people concerned.
128 (20%)	Other library "publications" for users: includes select bibliographies, accessions lists, library bulletins etc.
50 (8%)	External publishing, editing and (technical) writing (e.g. text books, journals and published abstracting services); public relations work.
63 (10%)	(Other) subject specialist work for the organisation – e.g. films, tapes, audio-visual material supplied; art work responsibility – production and reproduction: exhibitions and displays organised: briefing of salesmen: preparation of specifications.
36 (5%)	User education, demonstrations and social services to users generally, includes running user clubs and "book clubs" as well as providing courses and ad hoc instruction.
33 (5%)	News service, press cuttings, newspaper scan.
12 (2%)	Languages facility and service: translations and interpreting.

* Multiple answers possible in the detailed sector of this table.

As the group providing no extra services at all was so small (9%), there seemed little point in giving the full cross-analyses, nor in testing these for significance. A few apparent variations may however be worth brief textual mention.

Categories making comparatively lower non-routine provision were: minute parent organisations (18% no provision); societies and associations (also 18%); libraries (17%) cf. information units (0% no provision, or 100% provision); medical services (21%) cf. non-medical (6%).

14. Automation Potential

Why was the topic of mechanisation explored in such detail within the framework of an otherwise highly "people-directed" investigation? The relatively long final sequence of questions (concerning actual and possible access to computers and extent and type of usage) was inserted very deliberately as highly relevant to this whole study. It was not just a random or opportunistic exercise, aiming at incidental acquisition of trendy information.

Mechanisation potential and actuality were felt to be relevant to a labour-intensive occupation like library-information work, and to the wider context of the (post?) industrial society of the 1980's. The impact of new technology, present and imminent, on the whole labour force of the "developed" world is of current concern to everybody Or if not, it should be, if only for reasons of survival and self-preservation. It is of pressing concern to those employed in, planning or educating for intellectually based labour-intensive occupations – of which library-information work is a prime example.

Ratios based on the data we have collected in late 1979 inevitably lag behind developing reality. This statement is particularly applicable to the normative ratios. Doubtless the "ideal or optimal" ratios are also slightly coloured by this time-lag trend. To offset this – as far as possible – it seemed wise to collect information on the extent to which units already were into mechanisation, the extent to which they were theoretically in a position to do so (potential access to so-far unused computer facilities), the extent to which they wanted such involvement. When they have read the results of this sub-investigation of mechanisation, readers may wish to re-examine the ratios and revise the conclusions they have drawn from them.

14.1 Current computer access

This section is concerned with access, not with actual usage. It covers results of the first question on mechanisation; which was: "Do you have any access, actual or potential, to computer facilities?" Extent of access is shown in Table 63, nature of facilities and type of access in Table 64.

It might be more accurate to describe this section as almost exclusively devoted to access. An exception is made in Table 63, pre-empting a finding of section 14.2, by including a usage level column. Strictly speaking, this is rather an illogical approach to the material. It did however seem useful from the reader's point of view, to present access and actual usage side by side for easy comparison.

So Table 63 shows extent of access (and usage) not only for the sample as a whole, but for the sub-groups of the sample. Readers should be warned that apparent differences purely on the question of access between the geographical regions and between medical and non-medical services were not statistically significant. They are only presented in full for consistency and interest's sake.

Differences in access by size of parent organisation, type of organisation and service title were however highly significant statistically.

Full analysis of Table 64 by all the sub-groups of the sample would be tedious and over-large in format. Differences amongst sub-groups worth noting were: the larger the parent organisation, the greater the levels of onsite and offsite access to computer facilities – of all kinds. Industry appeared better off, as far as onsite access was concerned, than government establishments or

Table 63   Current computer access (and usage)

	Base* (100%)	No Access	Access	Actual use
Whole sample	655	209(32%)	446(68%)	301(46%)
Area				
North	144	54(38%)	90(62%)	65(45%)
Midlands	88	23(26%)	65(74%)	41(47%)
South	423	132(31%)	291(69%)	195(46%)
Parent organisation				
Mini	106	64(60%)	42(40%)	27(25%)
Small	151	45(30%)	106(70%)	65(43%)
Medium	225	55(24%)	170(76%)	115(51%)
Large	147	28(19%)	119(81%)	86(59%)
Size unknown	26	17(65%)	9(35%)	8(31%)
Type				
Industry, Commerce	277	74(27%)	203(73%)	132(48%)
Government	242	65(27%)	177(73%)	130(54%)
Society, other	136	70(51%)	66(49%)	39(29%)
Service title				
Library	327	129(39%)	198(61%)	127(39%)
Information	52	13(25%)	39(75%)	29(56%)
Combined	238	53(22%)	185(78%)	132(55%)
Different	38	14(37%)	24(63%)	13(34%)
Medical v rest				
Medical	128	36(28%)	92(72%)	70(55%)
Non-medical	527	173(33%)	354(67%)	231(44%)

* Percentages in this table run horizontally.

Table 64 Type of access and nature of facilities

Whole sample			Group with access %
655		Base (100%)	446
		Onsite	
216	(33%)	Terminal(s)[1]	48
68	(10%)	Mini	15
83	(13%)	Mainframe	19
7	(1%)	Micro or word processor	2
12	(2%)	Prestel[2]	3
18	(3%)	Nature not stated	4
		Offsite[3]	
124	(19%)	Terminal	28
7	(1%)	Mini	2
60	(9%)	Mainframe	13
1	(0%)	Micro	0
38	(6%)	Nature not stated	9

[1] Any of the other categories may theoretically be multiple, but in practice were less likely to be so.
[2] This is not also coded as a terminal, where only the Prestel terminal is present.
[3] Not necessarily own organisation's offsite facilities, use of nearby University or Polytechnic terminals or computers was encountered.

societies. Government services however did rather well as far as offsite access was concerned. Units called libraries were markedly worse off in terms of onsite, and fairly badly off in terms of offsite access compared with all other appellations of service. Medical services were worse off than non-medical in terms of onsite access, but better off in terms of offsite access. Possibly this "offsite" finding merely reflects the fact that medical services also tend to be government services.

14.2 Current computer usage

Table 65 Use and non-use of computer facilities

655	Base (100%)
194 (30%)	No access and no plans to get access or equipment
15 (2%)	No access, but plan to get equipment or access
77 (12%)	Have access, but neither use nor plan to use
68 (10%)	Have access, don't yet use, but plan to do so
301 (46%)	Currently use available facilities

Presentation of full results of Table 65 for the sub groups of the sample is not made on grounds of size and layout. There were however some apparent differences which are worth comment. Usage, like access, increased with size of parent organisation. Current use answers: mini 25%; small 43%; medium 51%; large 59%. Current usage also varied by type of organisation: industry-commerce 48%; government 54%; society etc 29%. So although industry-commerce and government had equal access chances (73% mention in both cases), usage of available facilities by library-information departments was higher in government circles.

Libraries (39%) and "different" services (34%), used computers less than information units (56%) and combined services (55%). But this merely reflect a lower level of access. Medical services (55%) used computers more than non-medical (44%), but this does not seem to be entirely a reflection of access, which was: medical 72%, non-medical 67%. Variation by area was minimal and insignificant. (See also Table 63.)

On the "no access and no plans", minute organisations had a particularly high level of this type of answer (57%) cf. large organisations (18%). This also seemed to vary by area: North 37%, Midlands 23%, South 29%. Societies had a high answer level (49%). So did libraries (38%) and "different" services (37%) compared with information units (21%) and combined services (18%).

On grounds of access, usage and preparedness to use, the following categories seem to be lagging behind: smaller organisations, societies and similar institutions; non-medical services compared with medical ones; services simply called libraries or called something completely "different" (although supplying information).

Amongst respondents who were making use of computer facilities for library-information purposes, how long had their mechanised systems or services been operational?

This question drew a poor response. Only 57% of the 301 current users supplied a start date or time period as requested. Amongst these responders the mean average was 3·49 years, the median 2 years, the mode one year or less. Specific answers ranged from under a year to 18 years. Only six services however reported possession of a mechanised system that had been operational for longer than ten years.

Adding this information to what we already know (e.g. that 46% of the whole sample were using computers and a further 12% were making fairly firm plans to do so) the picture now emerging seems to be one of relatively heavy but also relatively recent involvement in mechanisation.

To assume, however, that those who supplied time-operational data were "typical" of current users, or not unlike the 43% of users who failed to answer, is a rather presumptuous and debatable decision. Readers are warned that if we knew what time-spans, or even what reasons, lay behind non-response, we might see quite a different picture. Perhaps no answer was provided because involvement was so recent, the (non) respondent was barely into mechanisation. On the other hand no answer might mean a start date prior to that of the respondent's employment, lost in the dawn of library-information prehistory as far as that respondent was concerned.

Mercifully respondents were more forthcoming with usage details and descriptions than they were in terms of time. Under 2% of current users (5 people) provided no information about how they used computers in or for their library-information services. Usage categories as described by respondents in open-ended answers are shown in Table 66. They are arranged in descending order of mention or frequency of usage amongst the sample. The list covers all the positive answers supplied by respondents. In the case of the most frequently supplied answer "searching", it was unfortunate that it proved impossible to separate on-line from batch. Respondents did not, however, necessarily define which search facility they meant in their responses.

Table 66. Computer usage details

Whole sample		Computer users
655	Base (100%)	301
		%
196 (30%)	Searching: on-line and batch, includes one-off bibliography production.	65
161 (25%)	External commercial data base usage mentioned*.	53
83 (13%)	Creation of own data bases – e.g. inhouse special material or collection coverage. Includes thesaurus construction, maintenance and control. Material covered included patents, specifications, internal reports of organisation, trade literature, chemical compounds.	28
80 (12%)	Publications and services to users on a regular basis – e.g. journals, bulletins, SDI or current awareness services.	27
73 (11%)	Cataloguing and indexing, including union catalogues.	24
68 (10%)	Housekeeping: library-information routines and sometimes for organisation on a wider basis: membership, borrower, customer records; mailing lists; loan records, overdues and book location; periodicals control and circulation; document ordering; subscription renewal; library statistics, accounts, finance.	23
56 (9%)	Expansion (imminent or future) planned, extension of current activities and/or instigation of completely new activities.	19
19 (3%)	Specific software usage mentioned*.	6
15 (2%)	Novel or experimental – e.g. full-text retrieval; statistical calculation, calculating formulae, estimating, forecasting; user education and learner programmes.	5

* See list supplied in subsequent text.

Software received less mention than external data base usage. Software systems etc. mentioned by name were:

ASSASSIN	(2 respondents);
CAIRS	(3)
CROSSBOW*	(1)
KWAK	(1)
KWIC	(10)
(ICI MOND) KWOC	(2)
STATUS	(3)

External data bases used and mentioned by respondents were:

AGRIS	(1)
BLAISE-MEDLINE	(42)
BLAISE-UNSPECIFIED	(32)
BI/DATA	(1)
CAB	(3)
CHEM ABS	(1)
CHEMLINE	(1)
CONTEL[1]	(1)
DATASTREAM[1]	(2)
DERWENT	(2)
DIALTECH (TRC/ESA/IRS "RECON")	(30)
EURONET	(3)
GEISCO (physical property data base)	(1)
GEOARCHIVE	(1)
INFOLINE	(11)
INIS	(4)
LADSIRLAC	(1)
LISA	(1)
LOCAS	(2)
LOCKHEED-DIALOG[2]	(56)
LSE Statistical+Computer Science Data Bases	(1)
MEDLARS (batch)	(8)
OECD-NEA	(1)
PAS	(1)
PREDICASTS	(1)
PSYCHABS	(1)
QUEST	(1)
RTECS[3]	(1)

---

* "CROSSBOW Chemical structure searching".
[1] Via Prestel.
[2] Via this: Oceanic Abs., Rapra Abs., Biosis, and ASFA mentioned.
[3] Available in Europe from BLAISE.

SDC-ORBIT (18)
SRL Bayswater (2)
TECHSEARCH (DRIC, Dept. of Trade) (4)
TOXLINE (3)
UKCIS (2)
Unspecified external data bases-number (31)
of respondents mentioning

The list of external data bases is somewhat confused by respondents' own terminology and the level of specificity used to describe the data base. As an extreme example 31 people merely told us that they used one, either without giving any clues or in a way that defeated identification altogether.

14.3 Potential usage: desire to automate

Non-users who were planning to use existing computer facilities, or in absence of access to acquire hardware and use it in future, were asked to describe their plans. Answers from this sub-group of 83 people are shown in Table 67. Priorities were almost identical with those of current users of mechanised services (compare with Table 66). The main difference being situational. Potential users did not mention the category "expansion planned". How could they? As yet they had no ongoing systems to expand.

Table 67 Future plans of non-users

Whole sample		Non-users with plans
		%
655	Base (100%)	83
40 (6%)	Searching: on-line and batch	48
27 (4%)	External commercial data base usage envisaged*.	33
26 (4%)	Creation of own data bases	31
25 (4%)	Cataloguing, indexing	30
23 (4%)	Hardware to be acquired is specified*.	28
16 (2%)	Publications and services to users, on a regular basis.	19
13 (2%)	Housekeeping	16
8 (1%)	Novel or experimental usage	10
3 (0%)	Specific software in mind*.	4
4 (1%)	No details provided, although plans exist (too ill-defined as yet to air publicly).	5

* See lists provided in subsequent text.

The software potential users had in mind consisted of: ASSASSIN (1 mention), STATUS (1), TEXPAC (1). The external data bases they were considering using were:

BLAISE-MEDLINE	(5)
BLAISE-UNSPECIFIED	(4)
"BIS" (British Institute of Standards?)	(1)
CAB	(1)
CIBDOC[1]	(1)
CONTEL[2]	(1)
DIALTECH	(1)
FSTA (Food Science & Technology Abs. UK)	(1)
INFOLINE	(2)
LOCKHEED-DIALOG	(5)
PRESTEL-UNSPECIFIED	(1)
RINGDOC	(1)
SDC-ORBIT	(2)
UKCIS	(1)

Hardware acquisition plans concentrated almost exclusively on minis and/or on-line terminals. "We plan to use Prestel and an on-line terminal in the library during 1980–81". "Terminal to access Lockheed Dialog mid 1980". "Mini and Blaise terminal". "We hope to have a terminal for Blaise and possibly Ringdoc and a minicomputer for our own data base". Two mentions only were made of mainframe plans (one involved cataloguing). Microcomputers also only came up twice. One organisation was planning to share a micro with the "Admin. Department". The other organisation was planning to conduct "a two-year feasibility study of the use of 'hobby-type' microprocessor based computers to hold our bioengineering data base".

Respondents who had theoretical access to computer facilities, but did not use them and had no plans for so doing, were asked: "What would be your chances of using these facilities?"; "Would you wish to do so?". Results of these questions for the small sub-group concerned (77 units) are shown in Tables 68–9. Potential ability to use seems to exceed desire to use.

Table 68 Chance of using available facilities

77 (100%)	Base (non-users with access but no usage plans)
26 (34%)	Good
14 (18%)	Fair
16 (21%)	Slim
8 (10%)	Nil
13 (17%)	No idea

[1] Multi-national data base for the construction industry.
[2] Via Prestel, "Viewdata" system for construction industry.

Table 69 Wish to use available facilities?

77 (100%)	Base (non-users with access but no usage plans)
12 (15%)	Yes
36 (47%)	Perhaps
29 (38%)	No

Respondents completely lacking any potential computer access or plans to mechanise were asked: "If facilities were available would you wish to use them?" Answers are shown in Table 70.

Table 70 No computer access or plans – wish to use?

194 (100%)	BASE (100%)*
71 (37%)	Yes
60 (31%)	Perhaps
63 (32%)	No

* Excludes 15 people lacking access but with firm plans to get access or equipment. If added they would obviously all go into the "yes" answer category, which would then become 41% of a 209 unit base.

In conclusion, an apology to readers not yet suffering from that fashionable and prevalent disease mechanomorphosis, for the infliction of this final section upon them. Perhaps not however too grovelling an apology. Reality is ignored at our peril. Mechanomorphosis – or perhaps the right word is mechanitis, both terms seem applicable – is approaching epidemic status.

Some of the side-effects and symptoms seem worth diagnostic note. Rather a deplorable tendency, for instance, to regard human beings and the latest products of the new technology as interchangeable parts of the system. Eventually this attitude cannot fail to be detrimental to the interests of people, whether broadly or narrowly defined. So one hears managerial statements like this: "Before I agree to the purchase of this new equipment – how many staff will you be able to get rid of if I do?".

Instead of taking this line, the manager ought probably to be saying to the departmental head: "Before I agree to the purchase of this new equipment – why do you want it? What are you planning to do with it? What useful things will you and *all* your staff be able to achieve with it, that you couldn't possibly do before?".

In sane society conflict between man and machine is not inevitable. Conflict arises when men and machines are viewed as alternative labour pools or competitors for jobs. In such a struggle on such a basis man can only lose out – because it allows only a two-dimensional flatland view of man, as an inferior machine surrogate, inferior because fallible, expensive, etc. It ignores human flexibility, creativity and the self-programming facility.

Other views are possible and ultimately could be more profitable as well as more humane. Man and machine could return to a complementary relationship (the basis on which man has traditionally tolerated, even welcomed, machine intrusion to date). The machine should extend man's potential productivity at work, not compete with him/her for work. (Don't tell me that the world is so perfect already that it could not use this machine amplified personpower). Man-machine conflict in the context of the new technology can only lead to mass unemployment and ultimate innate poverty of the product (for which eventually there may be no paying customers anyway).

At the risk of sounding at once naive and cynical I would just like to make one comment on what seems to be developing into a sick and sorry state of affairs. What wonderful things we could now do with this new technology. What a wonderful world we might create. As usual human nature (greed, limitations of vision and imagination, opportunism, exploitative tendencies) is going to get in the way. But then, human beings do not, never have, and it would now seem never will, live in an ideal world.

So we hobble or leap, eagerly or fearfully (chacun à son goût) towards the dawn of what may very well be the "eighth day" of creation. Dutifully we march into this increasingly uncertain future, echoing as we go words attributed to the Deity by a current popular protest song: "Behold what I have done! I've made a better world for everyone." Any who demur, or contest this rash generalisation are all too easily dismissed as latter day Luddites. Let us pray that we are not finally forced to conclude (again like Ms. O'Connor's Almighty abstraction of "Man"): "Behold what I have done! There is no world for anyone."*

* Hazel O'Connor: "The Eighth Day" (Breaking Glass Album. 1980)

15. Appendices

15.1 Recruiting letter

3 Belgrave Square London SW1X 8PL telephone 01-235 5050 telex 23667

Director-General: Basil Saunders, M.A., F.I.P.R.

Date as postmark

Staffing levels and user

populations: survey

Dear Head of Library and/or Information Service,

In many other service professions (like teaching, medicine, pharmacy) ratios, both actual and theoretically desirable, of personnel to populations served are known. Information of this kind is considered vital in future planning for these professions at any level - national, local area, or individual organization. Ratio data have not been collected or collated for the library/information profession in its entirety (the exception within the whole being the public library sector).

The questionnaire you are now receiving represents an attempt to gather some indicative information about staff: user ratios in the special sector of the library/information field. This sector was chosen for initial investigation because it was felt that here least was known and results might be most directly useful.

We believe that this information could be helpful to managers of existing library/information units and to organizations contemplating the establishment and staffing of such services. So, we hope that you will be able to assist us and your profession generally by co-operating in this survey.

Results will be published by either the British Library Research and Development Department or Aslib. Individual identifiable facts or figures relating to your service, staff or organization will not be included in any publication arising from the project. Information given in response to this questionnaire will be respected as confidential and anonymity preserved.

The questionnaire itself is probably self-explanatory, but one point about it may be worth making in advance. Answers to some of the questions may involve the kind of information that not everyone has to hand, or can instantly and easily supply "from the top of the head". In the absence of hard data, an estimate or educated guess could be much more helpful to us than no answer at all. After all, this study is a first attempt to get an "of the order of" estimate of staff to user and potential user population proportions.

If, however, any answer you give is an estimate based on partial data, or a guess based on observation and experience, we also need to know that this is the case. So we would be grateful if such answers were marked with an E (estimate) or G (guess) as appropriate.

Hoping to hear from you.

Yours faithfully,

Margaret Slater

Margaret Slater
Deputy Head, Research.

15.2 Questionnaire

STAFFING LEVELS AND USER POPULATIONS: QUESTIONNAIRE
FOR HEADS OF LIBRARIES AND/OR INFORMATION SERVICES

1. TYPE OF ORGANIZATION

    Which of the categories listed below best describes your whole parent organization?

    ☐ industry   ☐ local government
    ☐ commerce   ☐ research or development association
    ☐ nationalized industry   ☐ learned or professional society
    ☐ public corporation   ☐ other (please specify)
    ☐ government
    ....

2. TYPE OF SERVICE

    (a) Is your service called (official title):

    ☐ a library
    ☐ an information service
    ☐ a combined library/information service
    ☐ something else (please specify)   ....

    (b) Disregarding official title, what is the best description of actual function or work content

    ☐ library
    ☐ information service
    ☐ combined library/information service
    ☐ information service combined with, or resulting from different activity (please specify)
    ....
    ☐ something else (please specify)
    ....

Queries to: M. Slater
              Aslib Research & Consultancy Division
              36 Bedford Row,
              London WC1R 4JH
              Tel: 01-242 4262

3. LIBRARY/INFORMATION STAFF

   (a) Please use the grid below to describe current staff situation and composition (number and type of people: include Head of Service in the count).

	PROFESSIONAL JOBS	SEMI-PROFESSIONAL JOBS*	SUPPORT STAFF**
Total people now employed in library/information unit			
People with library/information qualifications			
People with other qualifications (degrees, diplomas)			
Any vacant or frozen posts?			

   * Semi-professional: jobs with library/information content, but which do not necessarily or automatically require a qualified library/information worker or other qualified specialist.

   **Support: jobs with little or no library/information content; people following other occupations within the context of a library/information service.

   (b) During the year prior to receipt of this questionnaire, has your total library/information staff complement...

   ☐ grown in number
   ☐ remained the same
   ☐ shrunk

4. USERS (ACTUAL/POTENTIAL) WITHIN ORGANIZATION

   (a) What is the total staff complement of the organization/firm, employed at the same site as your unit? (All staff types - please include support and service personnel. Exclude however library/information workers of all grades/levels.)

   (b) What percentage of the above represents the potential user group of your particular service?

   (c) How did you define a potential user? For which departments or staff categories do you consider it your responsibility to provide?

   (d) What percentage of the potential user population actually makes use of your service, in any way at all and to any extent?

117

5. "OUTSIDE" USERS - MEMBERS

   (a) Are you a membership-type organization, society, association, institution?

   ☐ Yes   ☐ No   (If "NO" go to Question 6)

   (b) Is membership?

   ☐ mainly corporate
   ☐ mainly individual
   ☐ roughly equal mixture

   (c) What are the membership figures?

   .... within United Kingdom
   .... overseas

   (d) What percentage of the membership actually makes use of the library/information information service in any way and to any extent?

   .... UK members
   .... overseas members

6. OTHER OUTSIDE USERS

   (a) Are there any other outside groups which could - by right, courtesy or tradition - use your service? (e.g: hospital libraries and local GPs; bona fide enquirers; other branches of a firm)

   ☐ Yes   ☐ No   (Go straight to Question 7)

   (b) If yes: Please describe nature and (approximate) size of group(s) concerned.

   (c) What percentage of these people do actually ever make use of your service?

7. ASSESSING YOUR STAFF REQUIREMENTS

   Setting answers of Section 3 against those of 4 - 6 could give tentative staff:user ratios of various types.

   (a) Do you in fact use any ratio of this general kind when assessing library/information staff requirements or levels?

   - [ ] no never
   - [ ] not now
   - [ ] yes, we do

   (b) If answered "YES" above:
   What is the ratio used? (Please give actual ratio and explain how you arrive at and use it.) Does this method of assessing staff requirements work well in practice?

   (c) If answered in negative above:
   If staffing needs are assessed by completely different means how is this done? On what basis are calculations made? Does this method work well in practice?

8. STAFFING LEVEL ADEQUACY - NUMERICAL TERMS

   (a) Thinking just in terms of staff size (numbers) which of the following statements best describes the present situation of your library/information service?

   - [ ] adequately staffed to permit some expansion of services provided or to cope with increased demand if necessary
   - [ ] adequately staffed to maintain present level of service and meet current demand but any expansion etc. would be out of question
   - [ ] slightly understaffed re maintenance of present service provision and meeting current demand
   - [ ] really understaffed re maintenance of present services and meeting demand
   - [ ] other answer (please explain) ....
   ....

(b) What would you consider a comfortable but realistic number of staff for your library/information service? (include Head in count)

.... to maintain present service level without stress?

.... to allow for expansion?

9. ADEQUACY - QUALITATIVE TERMS

Forgetting number and concentrating instead on the kind of people on the library/information staff - are you quite satisfied? Are they the right kind of people for your service and their particular job? Answer Questions (a) - (c) below from this point of view.

(a) Which of the following statements best describes your staff composition

☐ all are above average, no complaints at all
☐ all are at least adequate, some of even better standard
☐ all are adequate or satisfactory, but none outstanding
☐ most are adequate, but some fall below this standard
☐ most are inadequate or unsuitable in some way, not quite what you would wish
☐ other answer (please explain) ·································
....

(b) If you have any current or recent experience of inadequacy or unsuitability - would you rank the following possible contributory factors in order of their importance as causes of poor performance:

☐ personality just wrong for the job
☐ motivation low or absent, lack of interest
☐ overqualified or underemployed in the particular post
☐ previous work experience or on the job training insufficient or lacking
☐ formal qualifications inadequate, irrelevant, or poor preparation for the work itself
☐ other (please explain) ···

(c) Any further comments you can make about influences on or causes of staff inadequacy would be very useful.

10. SAMPLE TRAFFIC RECORD

   It would help us a lot if you could pick any one convenient day of the coming week and record two aspects of library/information usage:

   (a) Number of enquiries and other requests for staff assistance during the day (include phone calls, letters, etc.)

   ....

   (b) Number of items borrowed.

   ....

11. "OUTREACH" SERVICES

   Do you regularly provide any of the following services to users?

journal circulation	NO/YES	(to how many people?..........)
current awareness service	NO/YES	(to how many?..........)
selective dissemination of information	NO/YES	(to how many?..........)
other active or outgoing services	NO/YES	(to how many?)

   ....
   ....
   ....

12. MECHANISATION

   (a) Do you have any access, actual or potential, to computer facilities?

   ☐ no (Go straight to Question h)

   ☐ yes, on site   (☐ terminal, ☐ mini, ☐ mainframe)

   ☐ yes, at another site (☐ terminal, ☐ mini, ☐ mainframe)

   ☐ other answer (please explain situation)

   ....

(h) Do you make use of these facilities for any of your library/information activities, services or routines?

- [ ] yes, we do
- [ ] no, but plan to do so
- [ ] no and no immediate plans

(c) <u>If yes</u>: What are they? Please describe briefly, including how long operational.

(d) <u>If no, but plan</u>: What are they? Please describe briefly, including when might become operational.

(e) <u>If no, no plans</u>: What would be your chances of using these facilities?

- [ ] good
- [ ] fair
- [ ] slim
- [ ] nil
- [ ] no idea

(f) Would you wish to do so?

- [ ] yes
- [ ] perhaps
- [ ] no

(g) <u>Again for no, no plans</u>: Please expand a little on your answer to the last question: either on purpose for which you just might wish to use computer facilities, reasons for not wishing to do so, or barriers to use.

(h) <u>No computer access</u>: If facilities were available would you wish to use them?

- [ ] yes   ) ....
- [ ] perhaps) Reason? ....
- [ ] no   ) ....

Many thanks for your tolerance, patience and co-operation.

122

15.3 Bibliography

(1) DEPARTMENT OF EDUCATION AND SCIENCE: Census of staff in librarianship and information work in the United Kingdom. London, HMSO, 1978.
(2) "LAMSAC": The staffing of public libraries: a report of the research undertaken by the local Authorities Management Services and Computer Committee for the Department of Education and Science. 2v. London, HMSO, 1974–6.
(3) LIBRARY ASSOCIATION. Commission on the supply and demand for qualified librarians. London, The Library Association, 1977.
(4) LINDLEY, R. ed. Britain's medium-term employment prospects. Warwick University, Manpower Research Group, 1978.
(5) MANPOWER SERVICES COMMISSION. Training Services Division: The provision of compatible manpower statistics. 1978. 12pp. (Unpublished, available on request).
(6) Organic change in local government (White Paper). 1979. Summarised and relevant comments also available via:
(7) HARDINGHAM, S. Organic change could mean £60m on salary bills. *Local Government Chronicle*, 23 March 1979, p. 311.